MOONLIGHT
SHADOWS
ON THE
WINTER SNOW

MOONLIGHT SHADOWS
ON THE
WINTER SNOW

MY JOURNEY OF HEALING
FROM CHILDHOOD SEXUAL ABUSE

SARAH ROSE KAIRN
&
JERRY PAYNE

Moonlight Shadows on the Winter Snow

My Journey of Healing from Childhood Sexual Abuse

Sarah Rose Kairn

FIRST EDITION

ISBN: 978-1-7354550-0-6 (paperback)
ISBN: 978-1-7354550-1-3 (ebook)

Library of Congress Control Number: 2020913678

A&C

Amelia & Christie Press

To the Spirit,
whose healing path
is illuminated
by the gift of caring people
who have listened, shared,
and walked with me
on this journey.

To all survivors of sexual abuse
and those who walk with them.

Alms

Like birds in winter
You fed me;
Knowing the ground was frozen,
Knowing
I should never come to your hand,
Knowing
You did not need my gratitude.

Softly,
Like snow falling on snow,
Softly, so not to frighten me,
Softly,
You threw your crumbs upon the ground—
And walked away.

—Anne Morrow Lindbergh

"May I learn to look at myself with eyes of understanding and love."

—THICH NHAT HANH

This is a true story. The memories and interpretations of the events herein are the author's alone, told as truthfully as possible by relying on detailed journals kept over the years.

In order to maintain and preserve the privacy of all of the characters, all names, and a few minor details, have been changed.

CHAPTER 1

VISION

The vision came upon me as I sat on the black and white shag carpet in my two-year-old daughter's room where she was napping in her crib. I slammed my fists into the carpet, but softly, so as not to wake Grace, and silently asked, "What do you want me to know today, God? Because I am going to do it." Then I became quiet inside, as quiet as I could, considering my ongoing anxiety and depression. It felt like fishhooks were tearing my heart apart in my chest. It hurt to take each breath.

The last time I was this suicidal, I was at a seventh-story window overlooking a paved parking lot getting ready to jump. I didn't go through with it then, but this time I was definitely going to kill myself, either by hanging or by carbon monoxide in the garage. And I needed to know from God why I shouldn't.

I knew my husband of five years would find a good wife and a good mother for our daughter. Tom would be better off without me. I was a disgusting and deceptive person. I hadn't been honest with Tom, and

I was a poor excuse for a wife and mother. Grace would forget about me anyway, since she was so young. I finally recognized that the long, lonely shadow of my life would always follow me. The illusion that I could pretend to be normal and bury the first twenty years of my life, like cutting off and throwing in the trash can the first twenty inches of a measuring tape, was just that. An illusion. A lie. The underlying tone of my childhood, as far back as I can remember, was sadness and fear. The fundamentalist Protestant God of my family terrified me. I knew I was going to hell, but I was in my own hell already, and the two people I loved most were mired in the hell I was living and now creating for them.

So I simply needed to end my life and stop hurting them. I didn't deserve their goodness and love anyway. I was unlovable. My family had told me and showed me this in thousands of ways, ever since I could remember. Even if I survived, I was destined to lose it all eventually anyway. I was now certain of that.

Robin had lost it all. A staff nurse and single mother who worked in the maternity ward with me, Robin had died on her thirtieth birthday just months before from breast cancer. She had been diagnosed less than a year earlier. Robin had few financial resources, and all of us on the staff gave her our vacation days, which the hospital converted into weekly checks that helped her pay the rent and groceries. The checks continued for two months after she died. We provided for her since her own family didn't. It was especially painful for us to know that no one in her family wanted Robin's beautiful three-year-old son after her death. They were not there for Robin when she was alive, and they were not going to be there for her son either.

Why had this happened to her? Why had this happened to her adorable son who was only one year older than my daughter? This is what made the connection, one I didn't make consciously at the time. But Robin's premature death assaulted my unconscious, causing my anxiety to rise to impossible levels. If she could die, I was certain to. Shame and guilt from my childhood overwhelmed me every day. I was to blame. My father told me that and it had become a part of me. My sinfulness was my ticket to hell.

Praying to God for a reason not to kill myself was a natural thing for me to do. The idea of prayer had come to me early in life when I said my bedside prayers. We went to a Methodist church—though my mother's family was Presbyterian, and my father's were strict Baptists. It was from these Baptist roots where I'd be introduced to Christian fundamentalism. But even as a child I imagined God as a power too big for fundamentalism to hold. I knew there was much more to the universe than what Sunday school taught. I loved animals, the oceans, trees, and flowers. Their beauty and essence touched me deeply. I found God in those things, too.

Winter, however, was like death to me. It was a day in February, that day I sat in my daughter's room and decided to kill myself. We were in the midst of another bleak Boston winter—gray skies with sleet and freezing rain, trees that appeared dead, scenery that looked as though someone had washed all the color out of it. And it was so bone-chillingly cold. It was depressing in its own right but doubly so in the haunting memories of my childhood winters. It was sunny on this particular day, however, and the sun was gleaming off the fallen snow and coming through the window of my daughter's room.

What do you want me to know today, God? Because I am going to do it. Then I closed my eyes.

That's when the vision began.

I am tied to a cross. No nails are used. There is an eerie darkness everywhere. I am outside in a barren landscape. There are no build-ings; there are no trees, no vegetation of any sort. There is no sun, no moon, no stars, no clouds, no color of any kind. But, through the darkness, I can make out others being crucified. Hundreds of people on crosses, a virtual killing field of unknown souls, but all seemingly in the distance. There is no noise—no crying, no moaning. Everyone is suffering in silence, each of us alone in our dying, too far from each other to communicate. No one is there to grieve for us.

I am naked. I am dirty and filthy, and I feel disgusting. I have a sense that I am two to three hours from death and I just want it to be over with. I am past anger, past fear, past caring. Whatever it is I have done, I know I am deserving of this fate.

In the distance, I notice a charismatic man dressed in a clean white tunic walking among the crucified. I know instinctively that this man is Jesus. Soon he is coming toward me, an ethereal light surrounding him, and I am suddenly filled with dread and self-loathing before this most holy of persons. I feel shame in every fiber of my being. I am tortured in my nakedness and vulnerability, and, as he comes toward me, looking right at me, I am terrified. What will he do? Will he rebuke me? Take me? Abuse me? He nears me, speaking not a word. The time has finally come. The judgment is upon me.

CHAPTER 2

PUZZLES

My parents never said much about how they met—or really anything at all about their backgrounds. This in itself says so much to me. What I know about my parents' lives prior to when I came along has been gleaned over the decades, mainly from relatives, answers to questions I've asked trying to piece together the puzzles that each parent represented to me. Information came in slowly. When I was a child, back when long-distance phone conversations were expensive, we had a five-minute phone timer. It was a mini hourglass sand timer and when the sand ran out, the five minutes were up and so was the conversation. Anytime I'd talk to aunts and uncles and cousins about my family's past, this metaphor would come to mind. I'd get a snippet of information and then the subject would be changed, as if the sand had run out of a hidden timer somewhere. During another conversation, maybe I'd get a little more information.

All in all, what I would eventually be able to put together was this: my parents were two emotional shipwrecks that somehow managed to find each other.

My father was born in 1924 to a dirt-poor family in Vermont that would only get poorer during the Great Depression. His father, my grandfather, was married four times, that we know of. Elliott Hollis was a stonemason, known for the quality of his fireplaces. He was born in 1876, closing in on fifty when his son Elliott Chester was born. My father would be called Chester to avoid confusion. Later, I would learn that a father's advancing age might increase the risk of Asperger syndrome in his children. To be clear, my father was never diagnosed with Asperger's. But it would help explain a lot.

Being in construction, I imagine Elliott's work was seasonal, and it must have been hard getting through the Vermont winters. Dad's older sister, my aunt Martha, tells me their small home had an outhouse, and water was retrieved by way of an outdoor hand pump. Dad had an older brother, too—Eugene—the three children being the products of Elliott and his second wife. Elliott started to expand the house in the late 1920s, but when the depression hit, there was no money left to finish the job. Part of the roof had been removed during the construction process and it was replaced by a tarp, which became the temporary roof above their heads for several years.

The kids attended a one-room schoolhouse, heated by a woodstove, where the younger kids sat in the front and the older kids in the back. It was the older boys' job to chop wood and maintain the stove. My father was smart, the smartest kid in that school. He'd be off playing while Martha and Eugene would be studying, yet my father would always do better than them in his schoolwork.

There were other things that set him apart. For a child, he had a remarkable ability to delay gratification. He worked as a paperboy, and he often did chores for neighbors, too. His brother and sister did chores as well, and every two or three weeks, they would all take the pennies and nickels they'd earned and visit the candy store. My father was apparently particular about his choices of candy. If the store didn't have what he wanted, he'd walk out without spending a cent. What child does that?

In the midst of the Depression, he was asked one year what he wanted for his birthday. December 17th, close to Christmas, it had been overlooked by his mother that year. There wasn't enough time to make anything extravagant like an article of clothing (presents were made, of course, rather than purchased), and so she must have been relieved when he asked for a squash pie. But then he added, "And I want it all to myself." I imagine the kids were always hungry back then, but my father's appetite was somehow stronger than his older, and presumably, bigger siblings. He'd always take the bigger portions of whatever food was offered, and his desire for a squash pie that he didn't have to share speaks to what I would later witness firsthand: an inability to empathize.

He had a business mind, always looking for ways to earn and save more money. This inclination would serve him well in his eventual career. But in the meantime, World War II came along. My father went into the Navy Air Corps in 1942 at the age of eighteen. The navy recognized his intelligence and sent him to officer's training at the University of North Carolina. He was ready to be deployed by 1945, but the bomb dropped on Hiroshima effectively ended the war, and my father's deployment orders were rescinded.

It was in North Carolina where my father met my mother. I have no idea how, but the one connection they had was music. My mother minored in music at the University of North Carolina, and my father played the banjo in a band. Did she see him play once? Did she introduce herself to him? Did he see her in the audience and introduce himself to her? Did they talk about music? We had a gorgeous baby grand piano in the house as I was growing up. My mother apparently was quite good with it, but I rarely saw her play and when she did, she would quickly criticize herself and stop playing. There was seldom music in our house.

My mother, too, came from a poor family. Her mother's family was from Cashiers, North Carolina, an unincorporated village at the southern foot of the Blue Ridge Mountains. Her people were farmers, living off the land. Of Scotch-Irish descent, they fished, they hunted, they grew their own food. When farming wasn't enough, they made moonshine with recipes passed down from their homeland. My great-aunt Selma's husband was killed by a revenuer during Prohibition. Widowed, with no means of support, and in an age before welfare, Aunt Selma got by with the food she grew in her garden and by taking in laundry.

Cashiers, though poor, attracted money in the way of vacationers from Atlanta and Savannah. In the days before air conditioning, wealthy people took their vacations where it was cool, either to the shore or the mountains. Cashiers was green and scenic in the summers. Tourists hiked and hunted and fished the cool mountain streams for trout. They played tennis and golf. My great-aunt Iris was listed in the 1910 census, at age eighteen, as "housekeeper," and it's probable she worked at one of the many charming hotels in the area. Later in life she would go on to run a bed-and-breakfast.

I visited Cashiers in the 1950s with my mother, sister, grandmother, and Iris. We stayed with Selma. My father was always working in the summers, but he would not have been welcomed anyway. Aunt Selma still lived in a ramshackle house where water was drawn from a pump and where light was provided by kerosene lamps. We went to the bathroom in her outhouse. The house was rickety, yet always clean. I remember a big wraparound porch and a lovely garden. It seemed everybody had a porch and that's where you spent your leisure time at the end of the day, talking with neighbors who'd stop by. "How is your garden coming along?" people would always ask each other. This was no idle chatter. The food that came out of your garden is what would help sustain you through the winter.

My grandmother was born in 1896 in Cashiers but somehow found her way to Asheville, where she married my grandfather, a railroad man. Interestingly, most of the men in my grandmother's family were railroad men, too. My grandfather came from a family of twelve kids, all raised by his mother. His father had run off with another woman. When my grandfather was sixteen, he lied about his age and volunteered for service during World War I. I imagine it was mostly for the steady paycheck, or maybe just to get three square meals a day. Or maybe it was just to get away. In any event, after the war, he eventually found himself back in Asheville, where he became a railroad brakeman.

A brakeman's job, in addition to braking, as the name implies, was to ensure the proper coupling of cars and to see to the switching of cars from one line to another. In the days before OSHA, the job was fraught with danger, especially the braking part. A brakeman would typically ride in the caboose, where he'd apply the brakes, but often he'd have to apply the brakes of other cars, meaning he'd have to jump from car to car. One great-uncle lost his legs when he fell onto the tracks. Brakemen ended up being the first responders with train accidents, too. These were the days before well-marked crossings. The brakeman would be the first on the scene. For the wives, I imagine being married to a brakeman must have been like being married to a policeman or firefighter. Would your husband arrive safely home each night?

My grandfather apparently had a temper. Bonnie Mae, my mother, was an only child and the apple of his eye. One day in front of the house, she was struck by a car driven by a black man. The accident would result in a broken leg and a stay in the hospital for young Bonnie Mae. My grandfather sought instant justice, running into the house and grabbing his shotgun. My grandmother chased him down the street and begged him not to shoot the driver, a crime he may well have gotten away with back in those Jim Crow days.

My grandmother got a job at Belk's Department Store in Asheville, and I presume she and my grandfather were able to cobble together enough to make a decent life for themselves and my mother, who came along when my grandmother was thirty, late in life for childbearing by the standards of the time. It's clear, however, that they wanted more for my mother than what they had, sending her to the prestigious St. Genevieve-of-the-Pines, a boarding school for girls that taught a college curriculum and added finishing school classes, schooling their students in social graces and giving a young woman everything she'd need to be a proper Southern wife.

My mother went to St. Genevieve from first grade through high school graduation and it must have cost my grandparents whatever savings and disposable income they might have had. Like most of her past, my mother never spoke of her time at St. Genevieve. I learned it from a cousin. I picture my mother as the odd-one-out at the school, a girl from a blue-collar family commuting daily to a school which boarded girls from some of North Carolina's wealthier old-money families. I imagine she was excluded. Was she shunned? Maybe that's why she never spoke of it.

I can only guess at what her childhood was like. I never knew my grandfather; he died a year after I was born. My grandmother suffered from depression her whole life. In the South in those days, they politely referred to it as being "nervous." After her husband died, suddenly of a heart attack, life would simply become too much to bear and she would sell her home and move into a bedroom in the basement of her sister Iris's bed-and-breakfast.

After graduating from St. Genevieve-of-the-Pines, my mother was sent to the University of North Carolina, where she majored in education with a minor in music. Sending a girl off to college was rare in those days. Somehow, she met my father, and then came a wedding in Asheville. The wedding and my father's plans for the future meant my mother had to leave school early, something my grandparents remained furious about for the rest of their lives. It's probably not a stretch to say my grandmother hated my father. She would later claim that my father was responsible for my grandfather's heart attack. He had worked so hard for his only child, saving and scrimping to put her through school—first St. Genevieve-of-the-Pines and then the University of North Carolina, only to have her drop out. For my mother's part, she would say she dropped out because she'd contracted mononucleosis in her senior year, forcing her to miss a semester, which she never made up. Either way, my grandmother and grandfather reluctantly attended the wedding ceremony, with my grandmother at one point arguing with my mother about her choice of husband and making my mother cry at her own wedding. Years later, my mother would make me cry at mine.

Neither of my father's parents made it to the wedding, either, although Aunt Martha came, along with a cousin named Lillian. Aunt Martha tells me that his mother didn't want to come because it was a "Southern" wedding. More likely, they couldn't afford to travel, nor, I imagine, did they own the proper attire. Either way, they would have felt out of place.

I came along soon after, in August 1947. A month later, my father started college at Bradley University in Peoria, Illinois, paid for by the GI bill. My grandmother offered to keep me, but I was packed up along with everything else. In the days before the highway system, we made the trek on bad roads and without the benefit of air conditioning. Cars weren't necessarily reliable in those days, either, and people didn't measure miles per gallon so much as miles per tire. Where did we stay along the way? Did my father find a roadside motel somewhere or did he drive through the night? Maybe he just pulled over and we slept in the car.

I'd have been better off in Asheville, and not just because of the travel. My father went to school full time, and, to make ends meet, my mother took a waitressing job at a lunch counter a couple of blocks from our apartment. All of one month old, I was left alone in the crib all day, with my mother coming home over her lunch break to check on me and then leaving for work again. My grandparents got wind of this and contacted the Peoria police, but, in an era before child protective services, where private family matters were considered nobody else's business, the police dropped the matter. My mother continued going to work each day, leaving me in an empty house, alone in my crib.

And so began my childhood.

CHAPTER 3

MERIDEN

My parents knew nobody in Peoria. They had no friends, they had no family. In my later work as an RN, working with postpartum mothers, I would discover research indicating that this situation is a known risk factor for child abuse. There's nobody to help, nobody to babysit, nobody to even lend an ear. Whom do you turn to if you're sick with the flu? Who takes care of the baby if it's all you can do to take care of yourself? Raising a baby is difficult enough but without a support group, it can be alienating and that alienation can lead to frustration and worse.

I would also learn that the process of infant bonding can be interrupted by a death in the family. The grieving process can pervade the environment, leading to an unintentional distance between parent and child. Six weeks after I was born, my father's mother died. He drove to Vermont as she lay dying, carrying a photograph of me with him. Apparently she got the chance to see the photo before she died. I was her first grandchild. I can imagine this scene playing out on her deathbed, a loving son sharing his ill-timed joy with his cherished mother, revealing her legacy to her before she passes away. So poignant. So touching. And yet I never heard my father speak of his mother. It was as though she never existed. Her name was Grace, and I didn't know this simple fact and wouldn't learn it until my daughter—whom I had coincidentally named Grace—was thirty years old. Nobody said a word.

I don't know how long I was left alone in the crib while my mother went to work and my father went to school. I imagine it went on for months. Perhaps a year? It wasn't very long ago that I learned about this state of affairs. I couldn't bring myself to go to my grandmother's funeral, but I visited her grave later. I stopped and visited with Aunt Iris at the time, and I asked her if she had any theories as to why my mother and I so obviously never connected, especially in light of the fact that she connected so well with my younger sister. Aunt Iris related the story of my being left alone in the apartment. Why hadn't this nugget of information come up before in all the times I'd asked relatives about my childhood? Did that hidden sand timer run out again?

My father graduated from college with a degree in mechanical engineering and took a position in Meriden, Connecticut, where we moved. Right in the center of the state, situated on the shoulders of the Quinnipiac River, Meriden was a bustling town, home of the International Silver Company; gun manufacturer Parker Brothers; and, up until 1940, the Bradley & Hubbard Manufacturing Company, famous for its brass lamps.

Here's the thing about my childhood: from the outside looking in, it must have seemed normal—a typical, postwar, baby-boom childhood. There were the standard childhood predicaments and embarrassments, of course. One of my first memories is of being made to stand in the corner for something bad I had done. While I stood there, I peeled some of the loose paint off of the wall to entertain myself. And I remember being in the backseat of our old, smelly black car one time and having my father pull over, get in the backseat next to me, throw me over his lap, pull down my panties, and hit me with his belt. I had no idea what I'd done to deserve it. His actions seemingly came out of the blue. Also, I used to suck my thumb and my father crafted a little metal cage that he put over it (I imagine the cage was probably a choking hazard). As I got older, some bad-tasting stuff was put on my thumb as well as on my fingernails. I cannot remember a time I did not bite my fingernails, much to my parents' and grandmother's distress. I still bite them today (much to my own distress). And I remember digging in the dirt with a little metal spade and pulling the spade straight up out of the ground and having dirt fly into my eyes. Somebody, I don't remember who, ran over with a garden hose and rinsed my eyes out.

Mostly I remember a new baby in the house. And the baby would cry. I would stand on a stool and put a blanket over the bars of the new baby's crib, figuring that if I couldn't see the baby, then I couldn't hear the baby. Much to my chagrin, not only could I still hear the baby, but the presence of the blanket had the effect of making the baby cry even louder. My sister Brenda was born three years after me in 1950. By that time, with my father working, my mother was able to stay home—and enjoy her new baby girl.

But normal childhood predicaments and embarrassments aside, life was full of potential. We lived well. My father's work afforded us a two-bedroom, one-bath, brick starter home in a postwar subdivision, populated mostly by Polish families of three or four or five children. We were the only family with just two kids. I made friends around the neighborhood. There were few cars and we played hopscotch and jump rope and kickball in the street. We rode our bikes everywhere. All the mothers stayed home, and so there was always somebody's mother watching out for us. It was safe and secure.

15

Some of my childhood bordered on idyllic. In our backyard was a brook that served as the rear property boundary. This was my favorite place to be. The brook was down a hill, about an eight-foot drop, and you'd usually get yourself muddy and dirty just climbing down to it. We would walk barefoot on the rocky bottom trying not to fall in, and I enjoyed the cool stream of water on my feet and legs. There were a few large boulders in the brook, and we would stand on them as though they were tall ships and we would play pirates. My mother, naturally, didn't care for the muddy clothes I might come back into the house with, but I quickly learned some elementary science. Should I fall into the brook, I'd spend some time on our backyard swing set, swinging back and forth and letting my clothes air dry until I could brush most of the dirt off.

Normally the brook only went up halfway between my ankles and six-year-old knees, but, if we had bad storms, it could rise much higher. Hurricane Carol hit New England in 1954, and the brook rose over that eight-foot embankment and ran a third of the way into the backyard. A gentle little stream turned into a raging river and I was amazed by the transformation.

On the other side of the brook was undeveloped land and lots of trees. My friends and I would climb the trees and make forts and tents and play hide-and-seek. We'd catch lightning bugs and grasshoppers. I loved being outside. I loved the flowers and grass, the trees, the birds and butterflies. I didn't much care for the seemingly ever-present mosquitoes and bees, but I loved the other creatures that made the brook their home—the tiny fish, the skating spiders, and the frogs.

When I saw a dead or dying animal, a frog maybe or a bird, I'd find myself struck by a sense of sadness over its suffering, and it was a feeling that never quickly went away. It was a helpless feeling, and it was somewhere in those years that I decided I was going to be a nurse. Another factor in that decision might have been the polio epidemic. It was frightening and, for a time, we hesitated to even go out of the house for fear of catching the disease. We'd see news on movie reels showing children in iron lungs and I couldn't understand why it was happening to them. Why those kids and not others? Why them and not me?

Outdoors, I loved the different seasons, the way the leaves on the trees wore baby greens in spring; dark, richer greens in summer; and then, in the fall, deep oranges and reds and fiery yellows. Our street was on a hill and during the winters, when the snow came, we would sled down the hill. I enjoyed making snowmen and at night, from the front window, I'd watch the falling snow against the streetlights, hoping for school to be canceled the next day.

Most kids hoped for this, of course, but for me it was no petty wish. I hated school. The days we received our report cards took me well beyond anxiety. It was pure dread. Report cards always meant a beating at home. I did poorly in school starting all the way back in kindergarten. I couldn't write my name and a note was sent to my parents. They were angry with me and made me sit down and practice writing my name on a brown paper grocery bag. I couldn't get it right and they became even angrier. I tried so hard, scribbling my name through my tears as my father and mother criticized me.

After first grade, my parents were told that I should repeat the year. I was one of the youngest in the class. My birthday was in late August, and the cutoff was September 1. I could just as easily have been in the following year's class and that's where I should have been. But my parents decided I should move ahead. To this day, I don't understand why this decision was made. And to think my mother was an education major! I went on to second grade, where I struggled there and then continued to struggle all through grade school, middle school, and high school.

My father tried different incentives, telling me once that if I studied hard and made good grades, he would send me to a private school with a girls' baseball team. I liked and was good at sports and so I told him I would try. But I continued doing poorly, and ultimately my parents had to pay for tutoring for me. This went on for years. My mother always seemed angry and impatient, having to drive me to tutoring classes every Saturday morning.

Sometimes I learned the wrong things. In third grade, I saw a word spelled out somewhere that I hadn't seen before. S-H-I-T. I had learned the "sh" sound by then and was proud to repeat the word aloud in school, where I was promptly told it was a bad word and never to pronounce it again. Undeterred, I wrote it in bold letters in chalk on the sidewalk when I got home. Word got around the neighborhood and the other kids' moms forbade their kids from playing with me. I could see the kids playing outside together, games that I was not allowed to join. I was shunned. With no support at home, I felt isolated and completely alone. There was now nobody. So I saved my allowance and the money I made from doing chores, and, about a week later, I put a dime on all the driveways of my friends. It was a shameless bribe, but it worked. Little by little, over the course of a couple weeks, the other kids began playing with me again, and I learned the lesson that pleasing others helped me belong. And I desperately needed to belong.

What I did like in school was art and music. In kindergarten we played the tambourine, the recorder, and the maracas. But my favorite was the triangle. I liked the delicate, high-pitched metallic sound it made. I liked that the sound lasted a long time. It was something like a bell, but lighter. It was magical to me. As I got older, I wanted to play the piano and violin, but my parents decided the clarinet would be what I'd play. My mother figured it would get me into the school's marching band. But I had a history of chronic ear infections, and playing the clarinet hurt my ears. I had to quit the instrument. In my parents' eyes—and consequently in mine—it was just one more thing at which I tried and failed.

I sang in our church youth choir. I enjoyed it and asked for singing lessons like one of my choir friends. My parents said no.

For a time, my biggest childhood problem was my sister. Brenda had access to the attention and care of my mother that I was denied. This was not just a resentful older sister's observation. Brenda was known by everybody as "Bonnie's baby." Ironically, Aunt Iris would tell me that she thought of me as "little Bonnie" because of my physical resemblance to my mother. When I look in the mirror, I still see much of her. Sometimes I wonder if this resemblance in some way helped fuel my father's behavior toward me. But Brenda was the clear favorite. Unlike me, she did well in school. And, any time we had fights, it was understood by both my parents that it had to have been my fault since I was the oldest and should have known better.

Discipline was always swift and severe. I'd be spanked across my father's lap (panties always pulled down of course) with a belt or hair brush. He was a big man, my father. Six-two and strong, with blue eyes and fair skin. If I cried, he would tell me he was going to continue spanking until I stopped. If I wasn't crying, he'd continue until I started. My mother's instrument of choice was a tree switch. Often I'd have welts and bruises on my buttocks and thighs and sometimes, when I was in middle school, to my complete shame, my mother would write notes to get me out of gym class so that the black and blue marks wouldn't be seen when we changed into our gym shorts.

Escape from my problems at school and from the harmful family dynamics came from summer trips to Asheville, to my great-aunt Iris's house. The first one, when I was seven, was perhaps the most memorable. For one thing, it was my first time on a train. We rode out of Penn Station in New York City and I'd never seen such an enormous building. So many people and so many trains and tracks! And I was endlessly fascinated by the sleeper car and the tiny sink and the way the bed came out of the wall.

Once in Asheville, I met my grandmother for the first time. She embraced me warmly, something I was not accustomed to. The last she'd seen of me in North Carolina was when I was an infant packed into my father's car bound for Peoria. "It's been seven years," she kept saying to my mother. "Seven years."

We stayed at my grandmother's sister Aunt Iris's bed-and-breakfast, a large and beautiful old colonial style home that her husband, my great-uncle Clifford, had built in 1925 when they were just a young couple. Like many Southern homes, the house had a big porch that extended along the entire front of the house, which helped keep the house cool in the summers. In the evenings, after the dishes and watching the news, we'd all head out to the porch. The adults would sit and talk while Brenda and I would run around the yard, playing hide-and-seek or catching lightning bugs in a canning jar.

Grandmother was living in the basement bedroom by then. The guests all stayed in the second-floor bedrooms. I loved the house but remained a bit creeped out by the numerous deer heads that were mounted on the walls in the basement—Uncle Clifford's hunting trophies. The eyes would follow me as I walked past them to and from Grandmother's small bedroom.

Aunt Iris was a wonderful cook. She'd been the eldest of ten and learned at her mother's knee, assisting and cooking for the whole family. Breakfasts, in particular, were unforgettable. Aunt Iris would be up at 5:00 a.m. to make a proper breakfast for Uncle Clifford before he'd leave for his construction work, and then she'd start getting breakfast ready for the guests. As you came down the center staircase, you could smell the warm baking-powder biscuits and bacon. Eggs were over easy or scrambled; you always had your choice. Sometimes there would be pancakes or French toast or oatmeal. The biscuits were served hot from the oven and the butter would melt quickly on them, and over the butter you could spread the biscuits with Aunt Iris's homemade grape or crabapple jelly, the grapes or crabapples coming from Aunt Iris's own yard. Aunt Iris made everything from scratch. There was always cake in the breadbox and often it was authentic pound cake—made with a pound of flour, a pound of eggs, a pound of sugar, and a pound of butter. Aunt Iris would often cook for social events at the Presbyterian church and adjoining fellowship hall, both of which were also constructed by my Uncle Clifford. Iris and Clifford were prominent members of the congregation.

Aunt Iris also had a large garden crowded with flowers and vegetables. She let me "help" her with canning and jelly-making, though I'm sure I probably just got in the way.

The differences between Aunt Iris and her younger sister, my grandmother, were stark. They didn't even look alike. Aunt Iris was outgoing and involved. She was active in the Church. She belonged to a sewing circle. She had her B&B guests. She was always busy and goal-directed and socially connected. Grandmother was dependent, isolated, depressed. I would learn more about her from Aunt Iris after her death. I suppose Aunt Iris didn't want to talk about her while she was still living.

Grandmother didn't have friends and engaged in few activities outside of the house. She was thin and anemic and frail, with arthritis and chronic back pain. To me, she was only ever known as "Grandmother," just as my mother never called her anything but "Mother." Up North, people referred to their parents as Mom or Ma and Dad or Pop. Grandparents were Grandma or Nana and Granddad or Pop-Pop. But there was a certain formality in the South. "Grandma" would not have been properly Southern.

Grandmother took medication for her pain and for her "nervous" condition. She never missed her TV soap operas, *As the World Turns* and *General Hospital.* She read magazines, but they were always movie magazines, and I never remember seeing a single book in the house besides, naturally, the Bible. A big excursion out would be to take the bus into downtown Asheville. Neither Aunt Iris nor Grandmother could drive a car, a not uncommon state of affairs for older women in that time and place. Sometimes I'd take the bus with Grandmother into town and we'd go shopping at Belk's and have lunch at the A&W Cafeteria. I always wanted to sit in the back of the bus because it bounced more, but I was told in no uncertain terms that the back was where the "colored" people sat. I was not to even think about sitting back there.

My grandmother was always critical, and she always insisted that I be a good girl. "Are you a good girl, Sarah?" she'd say. "You have to be a good girl." When I did something wrong, she would say, "Sarah, that's not being a good girl." I was glad she was not my mother, but of course I hadn't put it together that she was my mother's mother. And yet, oddly, I felt comforted by my grandmother. After lunch, everybody in the household would take a nap, and I would sleep next to her in her bed downstairs. I always felt loved and safe with her arms gently around me, something I'd never felt from my parents. One year, she went through her jewelry box in front of my sister and me, and she promised us each rings. Brenda's was a small sapphire ring, and mine was Grandmother's small engagement ring. We were to get them after she died. The promise made me feel special, knowing I was loved and worthy enough to be given something so precious.

At the beginning of every summer visit, we would take a trip to the fabric store and buy material that, by the end of our vacation, Grandmother, Aunt Iris, and my mother would turn into dresses for my sister and me using old treadle sewing machines. Grandmother had passed along her skills to my mother. By the time we'd leave, Brenda and I each had two or three new dresses. Not only that, we'd have matching versions for our dolls.

Back home, after our annual summer vacations, the rest of my childhood continued to play out. I fought with my sister constantly, though I remember the two of us sometimes peacefully watching our black-and-white TV together. We'd watch Woody Woodpecker, Hopalong Cassidy, Roy Rogers, and Howdy Doody. Once I remember Brenda and I seeing someone dancing on TV, and we started dancing, too. Our father was sitting in the living room and he watched us closely. His face turned red and he had a strange look in his eye and a smile on his face that scared me, although at the time I would not have been able to say exactly why.

At any rate, television-watching aside, the fighting continued with my sister, often taking place in the small confines of our shared upstairs bedroom. My father's solution was to build out the basement, turning part of it into a separate bedroom for me. Naturally, I was all for the idea. I even got to pick out the wallpaper. How could I have then known my father's ulterior motives?

The basement was where the gas furnace was and every time I walked downstairs to my bedroom I passed it and I could see the flames through the small, glass window of the furnace. The flames always made me uneasy. I started having nightmares around then, a recurring one in particular. I was in the bathtub and would get sucked down the drain, coming out in the storm sewers on the street. The street would be flooded, but soon everything would catch fire, the street itself becoming engulfed by flames, just like the ones in the furnace. I'd wake terrified and clutch at the cross around my neck and pray for protection. Then I'd softly sing Mickey Mouse Club songs to myself, and squeeze my teddy bear. I knew not to go upstairs to seek refuge with my parents; they'd only be angry that I disturbed them.

The cross I took very seriously and I wore it around my neck constantly. Around this time, I began learning about Catholicism from my friends in the neighborhood, all of whom were Catholic. In each of

23

their homes, there was always a crucifix hanging somewhere on a wall. As a Protestant, I'd been familiar with the plain cross, but the crucifix, with Jesus hanging upon it, touched me deeply. I couldn't understand why Jesus had to suffer so much.

One of my friends gave me a set of rosary beads that had broken. She'd gotten a replacement set and had no use for the old one. I didn't care that it was broken. I loved the rosary beads, loved the way they sparkled. And I loved the idea that each bead represented a prayer for Mary, mother of Jesus. I also had a "Miraculous Medal," the Catholic medal commemorating the apparition of the Blessed Virgin Mary to Saint Catherine Labouré, a nineteenth-century saint. I had found it lying in the grass around our house, as though it was meant to be found by me. About the size of a quarter, it was a silver medal of Mary standing with her hands open with love and blessing. The medal itself was on top of a larger, bell-shaped mother of pearl base. Silver ringed the outside in such a way that it looked like little rhinestones in the right light. The medal was heavy and beautiful to me, and many times I'd look at the Blessed Mother, feeling a need for her love and maybe even a miracle in my life.

I would often walk downtown with my friends, where we would go into the unlocked church, careful to cover our heads with Kleenex, per the requirement that women enter the church with a head-covering in those pre-Vatican II days. We would light candles and say a prayer before the beautiful statues of Jesus and Mary, their faces looking lovingly down upon us. Then we'd put our nickels in the box. The idea that our prayer light was still burning before Jesus and Mary after we left the church moved me. My prayer, along with all the other prayer lights, would still be before them.

My friends had what was called First Holy Communion. A celebration of their receiving Jesus, it was the best party of all. It seemed to me as if it was even bigger and better than Christmas. You'd get rosary beads, statues of Jesus and Mary and saints, and lots of presents and money. As a little girl, you wore a special white dress and white shoes and gloves and a white veil that made you look like a bride. I was sad that Protestants didn't have a First Holy Communion. My Catholic friends also told me that everyone had a guardian angel that was always with you, that you were never, ever alone because your guardian angel from God was helping you, no matter what happened, forever. The Catholic religion seemed much better than mine.

One of my friends gave me a comic book that explained all about Jesus. It had been created by the Catholic Church and when my father saw it, he became furious, grabbing it out of my hands and ripping it up in front of me. I stood stunned as he threw it in the trash. "You are *not* to look at this! It's lies and garbage!" he bellowed, although he didn't explain why. It wasn't a Catholic comic book to me. It was a story of God and Jesus and I had assumed it had therefore been holy. I was aghast at my father's actions. Needless to say, I hid my rosary beads and medal safely away. I had learned the limits of what I could openly share with my parents.

This was not the first time I'd witnessed my father's temper, and it certainly wouldn't be the last. My parents were frugal and I had few toys to play with, but I did have a little girl doll. Her eyes opened and closed and I named her Suzie. This was the doll that Grandmother would make the matching dresses for and so I always made sure we were dressed the same. One day, Brenda and I were playing beauty parlor and I took a pair of scissors and cut Brenda's hair, just as a real hairdresser would. When my father saw my handiwork, he flew into a rage. The punishment started with a paddling. It ended with him tearing the hair off of my doll, throwing the hair into the garbage, and handing the mutilated doll back to me. I was hysterical. I could not stop crying. Finally, my mother intervened and dug Suzie's hair out of the garbage and glued it back onto her head. The hair smelled like the garbage, but I didn't care. I took her and my teddy bear and we went to bed.

There was never any drinking in our house. My father, the strict Baptist, was a teetotaler and so his outbursts could not even be explained away by drunkenness. His temper was random and arbitrary and vicious. But, in time, when it came to my father, I learned I would have other things to fear besides his temper.

CHAPTER 4

MY FATHER'S WORLD

It took about two months for my father to build my bedroom in the basement. He worked on it on Saturday and Sunday afternoons. Saturday mornings he worked extra hours at his job and of course Sunday mornings were blocked out for church. So, on weekend afternoons, he built the bedroom while I watched and helped, holding nails for him or fetching tools. Sometimes he'd ask for the level, a fascinating rectangular device with a little bubble that had to be between certain lines. He sawed and hammered two-by-fours into a frame, ran the electrical wiring, hung the drywall, built the ceiling, and laid the floor tiles. I was captivated by the construction of the room, and, for the first time in my life, I felt special. After the main work was done, I even got to pick out the wallpaper: blue with white flowering dogwood trees. Eventually the room was furnished with a small bed, a bureau, a toy chest, and a lamp. There was a small cellar window in the room, too. But, being in the cellar, the room seemed perpetually dark and cold.

During the time of construction, my father brought a very large gray chair down into the basement. Its regular home was the living room, but he explained to my mother and me that it would be a good idea to have the chair downstairs to give him a place to rest. He could take a break from the construction work and not have to track dirt or sawdust into the upstairs part of the house. The chair was located between my new bedroom and my father's workbench. It could not be seen from the top of the stairs.

When he took a break, or at the end of the afternoon, my father would sit in the chair and ask me to come sit in his lap. The first time I was happy to do so, happy for the attention, happy that this special room was being built just for me. But, little by little, sitting on my father's lap in that gray chair became terribly upsetting and confusing. He would put a blanket over us and his hands would move under the blanket and he would start feeling me under my underwear. It was a secret game, he told me. I was not to tell anyone. Ever.

As the secret game progressed, he would take off my panties. I could feel his fingers, which would hurt me. He would smell my panties and smell his fingers. This was revolting to me. Why was he feeling the place from which I'd go tinkle? This was a dirty place in which you used toilet paper. In time, he would put his head under the blanket and lick my tinkle place.

If my mother called from upstairs, the game would abruptly end. But then it would start again the next time. Soon, every time my father worked on the bedroom, we would play the game. He told me repeatedly never to tell anybody. Not my mother, not my sister, not my grandmother. He made a special point about my grandmother. He explained that if I told, he would go to jail and I would be sent off to reform school. My sister and mother would go hungry and lose the house since he wouldn't be able to work from jail. I was bewildered. Maybe this was another kind of punishment for being bad. Except my father was not angry with me when we played the secret game. But I felt bad and I was always glad when the game was over.

After the room was finished, and I moved downstairs, the gray chair remained. A new one was purchased for the living room. The cellar chair was also where my father would give me spankings. Sometimes my father would come down to work at his workbench. He'd call me from my room, and, once again, we would play the secret game under the blanket.

It happened on weekends and it happened on Thursday evenings. Thursday evenings were when my mother was at choir practice at the church. My father would allow my sister to watch TV upstairs and he'd come downstairs ostensibly to tinker at his workbench. I dreaded Thursday evenings. My father wouldn't listen to me if I told him I didn't want to play the game. I didn't understand why he liked it. At one point, he started kissing me and putting his tongue inside my mouth. His fingers would be inside of me, and his face would turn red.

When I was ten, we moved out of the starter home. I left my Catholic friends, never to see them again. No more brook. No more woods. No more hopscotch and jump rope with the other kids in the neighborhood. We moved to a large, three-bedroom, two-and-a-half bath, two-car garage, colonial house in the exclusive neighborhood in town. When I would give my teachers my address, they would give me an admiring look that said, aren't you the lucky one? I'd cringe inside.

I tagged along with my parents to expensive furniture stores, where they bought new furniture for every room in the new house. My sister got a canopy bed. I wanted one, too, but I was told my grades weren't good enough. I was given an upstairs room with a window at least, which gave me a better view of the outdoors than my basement room in the old house. At nights I would pray by the window and look up at the stars. I wished on the stars, too, often singing, "When You Wish upon a Star" to myself.

The house was a sign that my father had arrived. He did well at his work as an engineer. The company he worked for built roads and highways throughout New England and points even farther away. For a while, my father worked on the Mackinac Bridge in Michigan. He was richly rewarded. He did just as well with his investments in the stock market. He devoured the *Wall Street Journal* daily and read every word of each stock prospectus he'd send for.

The new house had a large living room, the largest room in the house, and my mother's unplayed baby grand piano rested there. There was a fireplace in the living room that my father would light in the winters the few times we had company, which were the only times the living room would be used outside of Christmas Day. Company was sometimes my father's family—cousin Lillian or Aunt Martha and her husband Howard and their kids, or Uncle Eugene and his wife Marilyn and their kids. More often it was my mother's bridge club or gatherings of friends from the church. These were the only times my sister and I would be allowed in the living room, and then it would only be to say hello and politely excuse ourselves.

I would be reprimanded if I went into the living room to read, even though there were comfortable chairs and a big couch in there. There was a coffee table, too, and of course the unplayed piano, but there was nothing at all on the walls. In fact, there was nothing on the walls of the whole house. No paintings, no decorative wall hangings, no artwork of any kind. Not even family pictures. My father's concern was that nail holes in the plaster would depreciate the value of the house. There were never any flowers, either, due to my father's allergies. And there was seldom any music, no matter how much I begged for a stereo so I could play records like my friends did.

There was a formal dining room that was also off-limits, except for the occasional holiday dinner, or dinner party with adults of which my sister and I were never included, and of course for the times when my grandfather would visit. Sometimes he'd stay three or four months, and a cot would be set up for me in the dining room while he took my bedroom. There was no family room, and so the only places we could hang out were the kitchen, our bedrooms, the master bedroom, or the cellar.

We could watch TV in the master bedroom, and often we would do so as a family. My father would be reclined in the bed and my mother would be in a chair. My sister and I would be sitting in the desk chairs we'd bring in from our bedrooms. My father would be under a sheet and sometimes he'd bend one knee upwards and rest his other ankle upon it, making a kind of tent. Then he'd jerk his arm up and down under the sheet very fast, making the sheet shake, and his face would get beet red and then finally, with a soft groan, he'd relax. My mother would sit in her chair and never say a word.

Although we got rid of most of the furniture from the old house, the large gray chair came along and it found its way to the cellar, where my father's workbench was, just like in the old house. Our old sofa was down there, too, and a TV so that my sister and I could watch cartoons. But that's not what typically happened. My sister would watch TV upstairs while my father and I ostensibly watched in the cellar, sitting on that chair with the blanket over us. It would happen Saturday afternoons and then again Thursday nights during my mother's choir practice, just like at the old house.

On some Thursday nights, my father started the game in the kitchen. When my mother left for practice, it would be my job to load the dishwasher and clean the pots and pans. My sister would be in her bedroom doing her homework. While I stood at the sink, my father would get a small stepstool and sit on it beside me. He would slide off my panties and penetrate me with his fingers and tongue. I felt sick and paralyzed and I'd try to concentrate on the pots and pans. Often I'd stare out of the window above the sink, dazed, looking sometimes at the bright moonlight on the winter's snow, seeing the shadows of the menacing, barren trees, the shadows of some of the branches curved like fishhooks. To this day, moonlight reflecting off of a winter landscape creates a flashback.

In time, just the thought of supper on a Thursday evening, or any evening, would make me nauseous. I didn't have the appetite to eat at the family table. I'd normally eat my main meal at the school cafeteria. When I'd get home from school, I'd make myself noodles and butter and eat alone in front of the portable TV in the kitchen. At that time of the day, my mother would typically be out shopping or socializing with friends. Eventually, she would take part-time college courses at Central Connecticut State University to get the degree she never got at the University of North Carolina, a degree in education. In my room, I'd keep a stash of candy bars and potato chips that I'd buy with my allowance. I was never hungry for dinner, which, if my mother didn't want to suffer my father's rage, was served promptly upon his return home from work. I'd eat very little for dinner and often go to bed right afterwards with a stomach ache, even as I was accused by my parents of trying to get out of my evening dishwashing chore. Soon my stomach bothered me all the time. I became terribly constipated, too. My mother would administer enemas while my father watched.

The game continued. When I was twelve or thirteen, reaching puberty, my father would take me into his bed on Sunday mornings. My mother would always be downstairs making a special Sunday breakfast before church. She'd get a start on Sunday dinner, too, preparing the roast or whatever would be the main meal that evening. This would afford my father precious time. He'd come into my bedroom and get me, and, under the sheets of the bed he shared with my mother, he'd open up my pajama top and kiss me on my budding breasts, often leaving hickey marks that he'd insist I cover with makeup. He'd penetrate my mouth with his tongue, and, with his fingers, he would penetrate my vagina. Then he'd use his tongue down there. Sometimes he'd put his penis in my mouth and I would turn my head away and I could hear him saying, "Please, please..." Other times he'd roll me onto my stomach and something would hurt very bad in my rectum.

During this time, my sister would be sequestered in the bathroom getting ready, something my mother would insist on before she went down to get breakfast ready. There was less chance of discovery, of course, with my sister occupied. Was this by design? Was my mother trying to protect Brenda? Meanwhile, just to really cover things, the TV would be on in the master bedroom to perpetuate the illusion that my father and I were doing nothing more than watching Sunday morning television.

My mother would eventually come upstairs, walk in on us, see us lying side by side under the sheets, call us to breakfast, and walk out. Of course I could barely eat the breakfast she had prepared. I'd push the food around the plate and tell her I was on a diet. Afterwards, I'd eat a candy bar in my bedroom.

My father continually reminded me of the consequences should word of our secret game get out. But, by then, he was also telling me that the game was all my fault. I made him play it. "Look what you made me do," he'd say. "And besides," he would sneer, "You like it."

After breakfast, we'd all dress and get ready for church. We were a prosperous family and we looked the part. My mother only shopped in the exclusive stores and they would often call her when they received new merchandise they thought she might be interested in. She wore jewelry and furs, and her shoes and pocketbook always matched. My mother made sure my sister and I were dressed well, too, with matching hats, gloves, and shoes for church. My father liked this parade of his success. We never arrived in a car that was more than just a couple of years old, going, in time, from Chevrolet to Chrysler to Cadillac. My father was well respected in the church and he and my mother basked in the compliments about our clothes, cars, or latest winter vacation to Florida. My father donated money to the church and the ministers and elders would always solicit his advice on financial matters. One time, he donated more than five-thousand dollars to help the church buy a new organ.

When I was younger, I was in the children's choir. When I outgrew the choir, I sat in the congregation with my family. My sister would enter the pew first, then my mother, me, and my father. My sister and I were separated so we couldn't tease or pinch each other. What must we have looked like to others, this well-heeled, proper, God-fearing family? How could anybody in that congregation have imagined what my father had been doing to me just hours before? Now we were in church—God's house. I felt sick and I felt shame and I felt the fear of God and the dread of hell. Sometimes, if we were standing for a prayer or hymn, I'd have to sit down. I'd feel lightheaded and it would be painful to breathe. These were panic attacks, but of course I didn't know what they were at the time. Silently I'd tell God I was sorry and ask for forgiveness. The church service progressed around me. We heard the sermon, prayed in unison, and listened to the organ play.

Of the hymns we sang, a church favorite was titled, "This Is My Father's World." We'd stand together and I would try to move my lips to the words staring back at me from the hymnal:

This is my Father's world,
And to my list'ning ears,
All nature sings, and round me rings,
The music of the spheres.
This is my Father's world:
I rest me in the thought . . .

CHAPTER 5

ESCAPES

The dynamics of my family were best described years after my child-hood by a therapist knowledgeable in family systems. My family, she suggested, was like a solar system, with my father as the sun, and my mother and my sister and I as the orbiting planets. My father let us all know in no uncertain terms that he was the provider and breadwinner. He worked a full week plus Saturday mornings, and, in the late spring, summer, and early fall, he'd have to travel for work, often for weeks or even months at a time. This he never let us forget.

In addition, he studied the stock market and invested wisely to even better provide for us. He took care of the family car and he took care of the house, fixing anything that broke. We lived well and he let us know it. Parading us into church in our pricey Sunday clothes wasn't just to elicit the envy of the congregation, though it did that; it was also to remind us how well he did the providing.

I imagine it was also a point of pride for him, given his own background. His children would not have to live the way he had to live growing up. We were not to take any of it for granted, of course. My father recounted to us constantly the stories of his impoverished boyhood—the cardboard that he had to put in his shoes to cover the holes, the Sears catalogue in the outhouse that served as toilet paper, the lettuce soup for dinner. I assumed for the longest time that he exaggerated these stories. It was Aunt Martha, years later, who confirmed them, telling me in particular about the tarp that served as their roof for several years.

In return, we had to meet my father's wants and needs. My mother's job was to keep the house and family running smoothly. She was to organize the appointments and activities for us kids. She was to take care of us when we were sick. (Our father would never venture into our rooms when we had something that might have been contagious.) She was to have dinner on the table when my father walked in the door every evening at 5:30. On the nights when she was late, the verbal berating would ultimately lead to silence, the four of us sitting awkwardly at the table with nobody saying a word, although my father would occasionally interrupt the silence with another stinging remark or two.

The house had to be clean. No, the house had to be immaculate. My father, who had asthma as a child, had dust allergies. If my father saw dust in the air, floating, perhaps, in the glow of lamplight, he'd make my mother immediately drag the vacuum out to clean the room. More than once she had to do this late in the evening as the household was getting ready for bed.

This was the price my mother was apparently willing to pay for her life of comfort. I never saw my father hit my mother, but then again I never saw him hug or kiss her either.

Because my father traveled so much, he decided, prior to our move to the big house and perhaps with my mother's input, that we needed a dog. And so we got a German shepherd puppy, which we named

Morgan. My sister and I were ecstatic and promised to feed and care for him. We played with Morgan all the time, but he was a strong dog and one time he bit my sister, resulting in stitches. Morgan went to obedience school, but our father accused us of teasing the dog: Brenda got what she deserved. We were both sternly warned by our father that, if we teased Morgan again and he bit anybody, the dog would have to be put down. By law, he explained, a bite would have to be reported and then they'd surely come and take Morgan away.

Morgan was so strong in fact that taking him for a walk was more than we could handle. He pulled my mother off her feet one time and dragged her down the sidewalk. From then on, we simply led him out to the backyard and tied him to a tree when he needed to go out. On the few occasions that Morgan relieved himself in the house, my father beat him, first pushing Morgan's face into the floor where he'd peed, then muzzling him and dragging him out to the garage where he hit him with his belt. I never saw the beatings, but, from inside the house, I could hear the slap of the belt against Morgan's body and the pitiful sounds of his whimpering.

My job and my sister's job was to do well in school so we could "go to college and have a future." My sister did well at her job. I did not. I did poorly in math and reading. My parents were told I had ability but that I didn't try. I wanted to disappear when I was at school. I didn't have any friends there and I didn't have any friends in our neighborhood. Not like the ones I'd had in our old neighborhood.

What I did have were the trees. Not the ones whose winter branches cast shadows that reminded me of fishhooks, but the trees on the other side of the house, a grove of some thirty beech trees. Shortly after we moved to the new house, I asked my father if I could own them. He waved the question away with sure, why not? But I took it seriously. I needed those trees. They made me feel safe and secure. I hugged them. I never once received a warm hug from my mother. If she kissed me, it was only on the forehead to see if I had a fever when I was sick. The trees became my friends. I gave them names like Happy, Joy, Smile, Helpfulness, Growing, Brave, Healing, Willow, Friendly, and Singing Leaves, carving the names into the trunks. I talked to each one. Sometimes I would make a sandwich lunch and have a picnic with the trees. I would sing songs to them. I knew I could trust them and knew that they would never hurt me. Being amidst my friends the trees was a different kind of church. I felt surrounded by goodness and blessings when I talked and sang with the trees. I loved being outside. Outside was safe. Inside was where the danger was.

When I became a teenager, it felt childish and stupid to talk to the trees, even though I still had no friends. My paternal grandfather came to live with us one spring and summer. He took my bedroom, and the cot was placed for me in the dining room. My grandfather became my new friend. He told me how sinful I was and that I needed to be saved. He had me get on my knees and ask Jesus to save me, and he would ask me if I would say "yes" to Jesus as my Lord and Savior. He did this more than once. He read the Bible to me and taught me the fundamentalist view of Bible stories. Once I asked him if our dog Morgan would go to heaven. Grandpa shook his head. "Dogs don't have souls," he said. This made me cry, but Grandpa was intent on making sure I knew the truth. He would tell me to read the Bible myself and underline verses I thought were important and then we'd discuss the verses. This Bible study became the basis of our relationship. Grandpa never asked how school was or what other activities I might be involved in. It was just the Bible. During this time, I started noticing pain in my chest and painful breathing again.

We had household chores that we were assigned. We had to keep our bedrooms clean and load the dishwasher. I had to mow the lawn and feed the dog. Of course I had other duties to perform, duties the outside world could not have imagined. Between the guilt and the shame, the poor grades, the stomach aches, and the ongoing arguments and fighting with my sister, I mostly just felt sad and anxious. As I entered my teens, a familiar refrain around the house became *what's the matter with Sarah?* Asked directly, it always came with anger and exasperation: "What's the *matter* with you, Sarah?" I would shrug my shoulders. I wouldn't know what to say.

The guilt was such that I sometimes felt as if I didn't even deserve to eat—a further symptom of my emerging, insidious disordered eating. Certainly I didn't deserve our material luxuries. This would be confirmed by my father one Father's Day when he opened the card I'd gotten him and said, "You know, when I look at this card, I realize it's cost me one-hundred thousand dollars. That's what it costs me to raise you." I was one of my father's bad investments.

My father would relentlessly tease me. Sometimes he'd sneak up behind me and grab my arm and pull it up hard between my shoulder blades, hurting me. Sometimes he would give me an Indian burn, taking his large hands and putting them on my arm and twisting them in opposite directions. This would always make him laugh. Well into my teen years, he would continue to spank me, too, for getting bad grades or for fighting with Brenda. He would sit on my bed and pull me across his lap, take down my panties, and use a brush on my buttocks and upper thighs, insisting I cry or not cry, depending on his whims.

When I was twelve, a new girl moved in across the street. Diane was a year or two older than me and she was *sophisticated.* She dated boys and she played records on her stereo. She was thin, not fat like me, and she wore lipstick and makeup and nylons. She asked me one time if I wore a bra. No, I said. "Well, you need to tell your mother to take you bra shopping. Your titties are showing through your shirt." After I got over my embarrassment, I asked my mother if we could get some bras. She hadn't noticed that I needed one. Or maybe she had, but chose to ignore it. Once she decided my impending puberty was something she was going to have to deal with, she told me about periods and got me stocked up with pads. I began arguing with her all the time for nylons and heels and lipstick. I was the last girl I knew to get these things. My sister would get them just a few months later.

I also told my mother I wanted to go to ballet school. Scarcely considering the difference, she enrolled me in ballroom dancing instead. I hated it. Skilled as my mother was in the art of sewing, she made me an orange see-through dress for our class recital, sewing it out of dotted Swiss fabric, a material more appropriate for kitchen curtains. The dress should have been lined, but my mother felt that my slip was sufficient. And so everybody saw my slip, which seemed okay with my mother. Looking back, I wonder why she didn't simply take me to a dress shop. God knew we could afford any dress she'd care to buy. Years later, I would think of her as a student at St. Genevieve-of-the-Pines, my age back then, too poor to buy from dress shops. Did she make her own dresses? Did my grandmother make them for her—dresses that were fine dresses, but not the exclusive dresses cut from expensive fabrics that the other students surely would have worn? Was there a connection through time that somehow compelled my mother to make my dress for that recital? I looked like her, an adolescent copy of her. Was this a subconsciously repeated pattern? Whatever psychology was playing itself out, there I was, dancing with a boy and feeling everybody's eyes on me and my translucent dress. All I wanted was to fall through the floor and disappear.

Diane across the street told me how babies were made and she further explained how French kissing worked. I was aghast and felt sick. French kissing is apparently what girls did with their boyfriends. I had been doing it with my father.

The annual two-week trips to Asheville provided some relief in my life. For my mother as well, I imagine. Summers in general were better because my father was typically on the road, overseeing company projects that could only be undertaken during good weather. I discovered another valuable escape in musical theater. Even though music seldom played in our house, my mother had never lost her appreciation of it. In the summers, when our father was away, she'd take Brenda and me to productions of *Oklahoma, Showboat, Carousel, The Music Man*, and others at a summer theater in the next town over. I loved the shows. I loved the music and the drama, and the stories of characters overcoming difficulties resonated with me.

But the finest escapes were the summer camps. These started in elementary school with day camps with the Girl Scouts. I learned crafts and I learned to swim. We took hikes and learned about the different trees and flowers. Of course, I'd always loved the outdoors and I loved meeting new friends, too.

When I got a little older, I started going to overnight camp in the summer. The camp was in Stafford Springs, Connecticut, a cool, green, hilly place. It was an hour away from home but it felt like a million miles. You could smell the fallen pine needles under the warm sunshine, and the wind through the pine trees sounded like ocean waves to me. The camp was for two weeks and we lived in tents and swam every day and walked the trails and made crafts. I could never, for the life of me, imagine how anybody could get homesick, though some of the campers did.

I liked and admired the counselors who were always creating fun activities for us. They were college students, pretty and funny and cool. They seemed to like me, too, which always surprised me. For the most part, I was shy and quiet and just tried to fit in. I learned to paddle a canoe and row a boat at the camp. I was a strong swimmer and so I loved the swimming, loved doing something I was good at. Maybe the best part of the camp was singing around the campfire at night, beautiful folk songs and spirituals, everybody singing in unison or sometimes in rounds.

In high school, I went to Vineyard Sailing Camp in Oak Bluffs on Martha's Vineyard. The camp rested on the shores of a large lagoon. Martha's Vineyard was exclusive, even back then, and it was rumored that famed New York Philharmonic conductor Leonard Bernstein owned a home on the other side of the lagoon. This was the early 1960s, the same time that the Kennedys were on Martha's Vineyard. Some of our sailing counselors would race in the Edgartown Regatta. There were different races with different classes of boats, some of which were sailed by members of the First Family.

The camp was restricted to high school girls and there were two summer sessions, each lasting a month. Had it not been for our trips to Asheville, I probably would have signed up for both. We learned to sail in Ospreys, two-person sloops that were close to eighteen feet in length. We learned how to rig and de-rig the boat. We learned how to use a spinnaker, the large, three-cornered sail that billowed in front of the boat on a downwind tack. We did tip drills, learning how to right the boat if capsized. We learned knots, and right-of-way rules, and how to tack around to pick up a crew member who may have fallen overboard.

To me it was magic, discovering how to harness the wind to make the boat quietly glide across the water. There were life lessons there. I learned that although you could not control the wind, you could adjust the sails. You couldn't always go directly where you wanted to go. If the wind was coming right at you, you had to sail on an angle to it, but, by zigging and zagging, you could eventually reach your destination. Sailing took teamwork. There was a captain and a crew and they needed to work together or the boat would go nowhere. You had to be prepared. We learned basic navigation so that we could plot a course from one point to another. We learned to be safe. We couldn't raise sail before checking to make sure the life vests were present and accessible. Mostly, I learned you needed to be alert. You had to watch for other boats. Conditions could change in an instant—the wind or the weather—and you had to be ready for the changes so you could properly adapt.

The camp was on fifteen acres, and, besides sailing, there were hikes and crafts. There was swimming, and I would become a Red Cross certified junior life guard at the camp. We rode bikes, too. Rode them everywhere—twenty miles to Gay Head Lighthouse or to South Beach at sunset. We biked to church on Sunday mornings and sometimes the Catholic girls would come back from Mass, euphoric over a Kennedy sighting.

Like the other camp, there were evening sing-alongs at the camp-fire, complete with s'mores. Sometimes the sing-alongs were in the craft hall in front of a huge fieldstone fireplace. The counselors would play guitars and everybody would join together to sing.

When I left the camps, whether it was the Girl Scout Camp in Stafford Springs or the sailing camp on Martha's Vineyard, I was incon-solable. I would cry all the way home while my mother would tell me to knock it off. The fact is, people liked me at camp. We did things I was good at. One year at sailing camp, I was named Outstanding Camper. There were probably eighty other campers and the award came as a complete surprise to me. I never told anybody in my family, deciding it would be my secret. My parents would have stepped all over it, saying, "If you can do so well at camp, how come you can't apply yourself at school?" Of course there was one major difference between school and camp. At camp, my family wasn't anywhere around—my parents, of course, but also Brenda and that meant that for once I was judged of my own accord, not in comparison to my sister.

When I came home from camp at the end of the summer before my sophomore year of high school, I decided I wanted to learn to play the guitar like the counselors did. I saved my babysitting money and at two dollars an hour, it took me almost four months to scrape up what was needed for the steel string Gibson acoustic guitar I had in mind. But by the time I had the money saved, I found myself debating whether to spend it on a guitar or a pair of skis.

I had learned to ski at Aunt Martha's place in Brattleboro, Vermont. Martha had never really escaped the poverty from which her and my father had come, although things were certainly not as grim as her childhood days. She and my Uncle Howard and their two sons—our cousins Matthew, a year younger than me, and Luke, the same age as Brenda— lived in the upstairs apartment of Howard's mother's home, a small, turn-of-the-century Victorian house that was a stripped-down version of the more elaborate Victorians of its day. There was a kerosene heater in the living room and a kerosene stove in the kitchen and that's all that provided warmth for the family in the bitter Vermont winters. Howard had gone deaf as an adult, the result of a strep infection. He wore a rudimentary hearing aid that never seemed to help and he could only get work as a janitor. My father had given them our 1959 Chevy Station Wagon when he'd upgraded to his Chrysler and they were forever grateful to him for that. My aunt admired her brother greatly for his success, even adored him.

When we'd visit them in the winters, Matthew and Luke and Brenda and I would ski down the hill that constituted their back yard. Our cousins had learned to ski in school. It was part of the physical education program, part of the culture, really. Every kid skied. Equipment was made available as part of a ski swap program with donated skis and boots and poles, which is how Matthew and Luke were able to participate. We'd ski all day down the backyard hill. At nights Brenda and I were consigned to an unheated porch where our beds were. We slept with our hats on and I felt like a piece of cheese sandwiched between the mattress and the multiple layers of heavy blankets.

Our mother never came along on the trips to Vermont, electing to stay at home for the peace and quiet, I presume. In Vermont, my father would take the four of us kids to Mount Snow and Stratton Mountain to ski. I loved it. I loved the ski lifts with the panoramic views of the mountains, the trees covered with sparkling white snow, the clear blue skies and the cold fresh air. I loved shushing down the slopes and I became good at it, giving me a feeling of accomplishment like what I'd felt at the camps.

So I was torn between skis and a guitar, but ultimately decided I'd get more use out of a guitar. And then my father made the decision even easier that Christmas when my sister and I each found a pair of skis under the tree, a rare instance of me getting something I really wanted. I bought the Gibson and a music book and taught myself to play. I learned the basic chords and practiced until I got the requisite calluses on my fingers. I'd play alone in my bedroom and sing out loud and be transported to those wonderful, warm summer evenings at camp, away from home—the happiest times of my life.

CHAPTER 6

CORE DARKNESS

I had only one date as a teenager. It happened while my father was traveling. When he returned and discovered I'd been out with a boy, he told my mother and me that I could not date anymore. He was concerned about what a boy might do to me.

Not dating was just one more thing that seemed to separate me from my classmates. I didn't go to the junior or senior proms. I was athletic, but there were no team sports to speak of for girls back in those days. I'd outgrown the church choir and the Girl Scouts only met once a month. I had no sense of belonging. I spent high school trying to survive as best I could, knowing I would always be the odd one out. I'd never be one of the cool kids and I'd never go out with a sports jock. Meanwhile, my class work was getting no better. My French teacher was willing to pass me with a D, so long as I promised never to take a language class again. High school had become a continuation of the nightmare that was my life and it was getting more and more intolerable.

At home, the fights I was having with my sister became rougher, complete with slapping, punching, shoving, and pulling hair. But I was getting stronger. I was five-foot-seven and 170 pounds, and the biking, skiing, and swimming were making me a tougher threat. Soon enough, Brenda started giving me more respect and distance and stopped whining and tattling on me to our mother.

I also knew that I was becoming strong enough to stand up to my father's abuse. Though I didn't date, I heard what other kids were doing on dates and it sickened me to know it was the same stuff I'd been doing with my father. I had no definite plan on how exactly to stop the abuse, but I knew that I was going to. Thankfully, there were no guns in the house. I can't say for certain, but, looking back, had a gun been available to me, I might well have used it to shoot my father dead.

The abuse ended without bloodshed one night while my mother was off at choir practice and Brenda was at a friend's house. I was fifteen. My father came after me. "You disgust me!" I yelled as I pushed him away. He became enraged and came at me with more force, grabbing at my shirt, which tore completely off as I ran from him to my bedroom. I slammed the door behind me and locked it. My father went to get a coat hanger to pick the lock, and, when I heard him outside the door, I went over to the window and opened it, feeling the cold winter air rushing in. I knew my father heard the window opening and I yelled through the door to him, "I'm taking the rest of my clothes off now! If you come in that door, I am going to jump naked out of the window!"

My father knew it was no idle threat. I was ready to do it, and, to this day, I sometimes wish I had, just to listen to my father— this respected man in our exclusive neighborhood, this pillar of the church—try to explain to the neighbors why his daughter had jumped naked out of her second-story bedroom window while he was alone in the house with her. And then have to further explain it to the doctor had I hurt myself. Somebody may have asked for my side of the story, and maybe they'd have believed me. Maybe my mother would no longer have been able to ignore what had been going on under her roof. If I hadn't been hurt, I'd have run across the street to Diane's house, where I'd ask for a blanket and spill the secrets of our house to her and her parents. At the time, of course, I was still laboring under the assumption that I'd been guilty, too. I was sure I'd be sent to reform school once the whole sordid story got out, but I didn't care. The mask would have been ripped off our oh-so-perfect life. Something would have changed. I knew it, and my father knew it. And he had more to lose.

My father walked away from the door and he never molested me again. The spanking stopped as well. I kept my distance from him, however, and never stayed with him in the same room alone. I played defense. If he called me to the cellar, I thought up an excuse not to go down there and instead I'd go into my room and lock the door. If I was in the kitchen with both my mother and father, and my mother would leave, I'd leave too. I became hyperaware of my surroundings. I stayed locked in my room on the evenings when my mother would go to choir practice. I'd get into my pajamas, which were easier to slip out of so that I could fulfill my threat of jumping naked from the window. That threat must have remained clear in my father's mind because he never tried anything again. Years before he had taught me to play chess and he'd never once lost to me. But this time—perhaps—I had him in checkmate.

I stopped the abuse, presumably, but my sense of isolation contin-ued to grow. From that time forward, I remained mostly in my room with the door locked, grateful for my guitar to keep me company. Eventually I thought about running away, possibly to New York City, which was only a two-hour bus ride. My sailing experience kicked in and I remembered how important preparation was. How could I make the trip safely? What would I do in case of emergency? And what would I do when I got there? I had no answers to these questions. I knew nobody in New York. I didn't even have a high school diploma. What kind of job could I get? Where would I live? Who could I trust? I knew I could always become a prostitute, but decided not to trade one nightmare for another.

Where else could I go? I couldn't tell my secret to anyone, and so there was no way I could ask my grandmother or Aunt Iris if I could live with them. Naturally, they'd want to know why. What would I tell them? Ultimately, there was nothing to do but stay.

With nobody to talk to and nowhere to turn, I found some solace in popular evangelist Billy Graham. He was on TV regularly and his ministry was offering helpful books for five-dollar donations. I gave myself to Jesus again and ordered a book to help me with my new life with Him. I wrote a long letter that I sent with my money, telling Reverend Graham that I didn't get along with my family and that I wanted to run away from home. I asked him to send me the book he thought would help me the most. A couple of weeks later, I received a package of six books in the mail, along with an encouraging letter from somebody in the Billy Graham ministry.

The books from Billy Graham initially helped, but my problems weren't going away. When I stopped my father's sexual abuse, I assumed I would automatically move beyond it. The abuse would now be a part of my past, to be forgotten and left behind. But stopping the abuse didn't stop the misery in my head. I felt as if I was being smothered by it. Ironically, stopping the abuse actually reinforced the idea that it had been my fault. If I had the power to stop it, why hadn't I done so earlier? I felt guilty. I felt despicable and vile. Surely if my secret ever got out, I'd be shunned, considered worthy only of jail or death. Meanwhile, my father was revered. I could sense the adoration from others in the way they looked at him and spoke to him. He was wealthy, smart, and hardworking. A charitable man. And a wonderful provider. *What's the matter with you, Sarah?*

The loneliness and isolation became unbearable. So did living a life that was essentially a lie. I possessed some kind of core darkness, I was certain of it. I couldn't allow anybody to see that. They only saw the mask I wore and the life I pretended to live. And then of course there was the thought that maybe some night, when my mother and sister were out of the house, my father might break into my room and attack me before I could get to the window.

It was all more than I could take, and, one night, I sat down and wrote a suicide note, saying I knew I was unloved and that I could not go on. I mentioned my father in the note. I wrote that I wished he was more like Mr. Johnson, my chemistry teacher, who was kind and helpful to me, even though I struggled in his class. I wasn't even thinking about the sexual abuse. I just wanted a father who was nice to me.

I placed the note on my dresser. My plan was to overdose on pills. All I could find were aspirin, but I imagined they would do the job. There were ten left in the bottle and I took them all. Almost immediately I regretted it. Death, it suddenly occurred to me, would mean going to hell, for surely, that's where I was headed. I had a panic attack. I was sick with fear. I was also sick from the aspirin, which were doing nothing but giving me a horrible stomach ache. I lay awake most of the night, nauseous and terrified about where I was going to spend my eternal life. Finally, around 4:00 a.m., I realized I was not going to die. More importantly, I realized I was not, at least for the time being, going to hell, and I was overcome with relief. Two hours later, the alarm went off and I went to school like it was any other day.

I'd forgotten, in the meantime, about the note, leaving it on the dresser. My mother must have found it cleaning my room because when I came home that night, it was gone. Nobody ever mentioned it to me, but maybe my mother said something about it to my father.

One Saturday morning, I was sitting in my room with the door ajar. My mother was in the master bedroom, vacuuming and dusting, and I knew she'd be doing my room next. My father walked in and sat down next to me on the bed, telling me he had something important to tell me. In a calm, quiet voice I could hear above the sound of the vacuum down the hall, he said, "I'm sorry for having been a little fresh with you, Sarah. Can you forgive me?" Since I was trying to be a good Christian, I told him yes. Then he walked out of my room and my mother came in shortly afterwards to vacuum and dust.

CHAPTER 7

TIRED OF LIVING

I wasn't going to hell, but then I wasn't going anywhere else, either. I couldn't go to New York, I couldn't run away to Asheville, and I couldn't kill myself. The words of *Showboat*'s "Old Man River" echoed in my head: I was "tired of living, but scared of dying."

By my junior year of high school, I was thinking of life beyond our house. I couldn't wait to leave home. But I knew I wasn't college material, so where was I headed? How was I going to support myself as an adult? In the back of my mind remained the idea of becoming a nurse, the idea that had been with me since I was a little girl. For as long as I could remember, I had been struck by the suffering of animals and people, and I thought, in my own small way, perhaps I could work toward the relief of such suffering. I started taking my tutoring, which had continued through high school, more seriously. I had a goal now: to become a registered nurse.

I sent away for catalogues for nursing schools, and, in my senior year, I began applying, focusing only on schools that were out of state.

Schools in Massachusetts and New York seemed far enough away without being too far. With my mediocre grades of C's, the occasional B-minus, and D's in math, it wasn't easy, but eventually Albany Medical Center School of Nursing in Albany, New York, accepted me for their March class. The acceptance came with a condition. I would need to take tutoring in Albany first, and then pass the nursing school entrance exam.

I graduated high school in June of 1965. My father was called away for a work emergency and was unable to attend the commencement. My mother and sister came. Afterwards, while my schoolmates' parents were holding graduation parties or taking their kids to posh restaurants for celebratory dinners, my mother took Brenda and me to Friendly's for hamburgers.

Not long after graduation, I went to Vineyard Sailing Camp again, this time as a counselor-in-training. That year, it occurred to me that once I was out in the real world, life might be a lot more like camp than what I'd experienced at home or in school. I'd meet new people, make friends, and enjoy my newfound freedom. After camp was our summer trip to Asheville, and, by the end of August, when I left home for Albany to enroll in the tutoring, I was getting excited by the prospects of a new life.

My wealthy Aunt Lillian was going to pay for my tuition. I would not be beholden to my father for it. Lillian was a cousin of my father's, and she would generously pay for the education of Uncle Eugene's three children, Aunt Martha's two children, and Brenda and me. Lillian's father had been the successful owner of hardware stores in North Haven and New Haven, Connecticut. She was around five feet tall and on the stout side. For all her money, she was a bit frumpy in her manner of dress, all the way down to her old-lady shoes. She lived in a large, beautiful Victorian house in North Haven that her brother Homer, an architect and Yale grad, had designed. She never put the heat above sixty-seven, even on the coldest winter day, a consequence of her frugal, New England sensibility. We knew not to go to Lillian's house without bringing along heavy sweaters.

The house rested on ten acres of land that bordered the Housatonic River. There was a stunning view of the river from a large bay window in the dining room. There was a wonderful wraparound porch for summer comfort back in the days before air conditioning. There were three fireplaces in the house, one in the parlor that connected to the music room, one in the dining room, and one in the upstairs master bedroom. There were two large Tiffany windows ordered from New York that gave light to the main staircase. Gorgeous Oriental rugs were everywhere, as well as original paintings and valuable antiques. On the property was a large carriage house that had been converted to a garage, with four cars and space left over for storage. Lillian drove a huge 1953 Buick, green with a white top.

Lillian never married and never needed to work. She was a "society" woman, and spent her time volunteering at her church and local charities. She also took long cruises to South America and Europe and elsewhere. I remember as a child my father driving us all to New York City with Lillian so that she could board a ship bound for India.

We would often visit Lillian for Sunday dinners, or she would visit us. Holiday gatherings were frequently held at her house, with Uncle Eugene and Aunt Marilyn and their kids. These were elegant occasions. The silver place settings extended far to the right and to the left, with dessert spoons and salad forks and individual butter knives. Beautiful crystal and china were standard, and we kids had to be careful not to break anything. I remember having to wait until I was old enough to have tea, which seemed very sophisticated to me.

Lillian owned the first television I had ever seen in a person's home, and it was housed in a gorgeous wood cabinet. She had a beautiful antique piano, too, and a large American flag from the 1860s with thirty-six stars that she would hang outside every Fourth of July. She fed the birds in the winter and had feeders near her kitchen window and I learned about birds from her; she knew every kind that made an appearance and how to feed them.

Lillian became an important figure for me, maybe every bit as important as Aunt Iris in Asheville. Lillian was insightful enough to see the family dynamics for what they were. She knew that "Bonnie's baby" was Brenda. She cared about me, one of the few people in the world who did, so far as I could tell. My birthday was always close to Labor Day, and, at the end of every summer, Aunt Lillian would have a combination Labor Day/ birthday party, knowing I could never expect my parents to throw a party for me. There was always a beautiful cake and festive hats and noisemakers.

With the promise that tuition would be taken care of by Aunt Lillian, I left for Albany, landing at the YWCA, where I rented a single room with a shared bath. A buffet dinner was available Mondays through Fridays for a little extra, or you could make use of the kitchen. There was a common refrigerator in the kitchen, and there were little security cages for each resident so you could lock up your food. Such was my naiveté that I could not understand why anyone would need to do that until someone explained to me that locking up your food would keep others from stealing it.

I'd need to pay my own rent and so I took a job as a ward secretary on the pediatric floor of Albany Medical Center. Then I started taking the required tutoring I would need to get into nursing school the following spring. Two evenings a week I met with the tutor to study remedial math and science and reading.

I had never learned to drive, and had no car anyway, so I took the bus to the hospital every day. On nice days, especially in the spring, I would walk home. It was a four-mile walk from the hospital, and I would often stop along the way at a Catholic church, where I would light a candle and pray for help and guidance.

I knew nobody in Albany, and, in my spare time, I would sit in my room at the Y and listen to records on the record player I had bought for myself. I couldn't afford a proper stereo, but the room was small, and the record player was sufficient. I started eating a lot. On days off, increasingly lonely and with nothing to do and nobody to visit, I would stop at the donut shop and buy a dozen donuts, often eating six or seven at a time. Not surprisingly, I put on weight, eventually topping out at 195 pounds before starting nursing school.

To curtail the loneliness, I offered to work overtime. As a ward secretary, I often had to work weekends and holidays anyway, and that was fine by me. I liked it at the hospital. I looked at the nurses with envy. The student nurses wore their crisp white uniforms with pink sleeves, nylons, white shoes, and caps, and I couldn't wait to become one of them. On holidays I'd get time and a half. You had to work either Thanksgiving or Christmas, and you'd get the other holiday off. I went home for Thanksgiving that year, taking the bus back to Meriden, my parents never offering to come pick me up. In fact, they declined to send me bus fare, and I had to pay for the trip myself. At Christmas, I was happy to stay in Albany and work.

March finally came around and I passed the entrance exam and started nursing school, moving from my room at the Y to a dorm on the hospital campus. There were about sixty of us in the class. We all received our books and uniforms and began taking classes in subjects like anatomy and microbiology. We learned about abnormal physiology, studying about disease. For the first three months, we were kept out of the clinical area of the hospital, but we nevertheless started learning some of the basic nursing skills—how to make beds, give baths, take blood pressure, administer injections.

The dorms were fun, and I became part of a group of four friends. One of them had a car, and in our spare time we'd go sightseeing or shopping or to a movie. Sometimes we'd get out of the city and go on a picnic and take nature walks.

In class, I noticed it took me longer to learn things than it took the other students, but I decided that that was okay. I knew that the learning would come, and I gave myself permission to take the time I needed. Maybe I'd have to work harder than the other students to finish everything by a certain deadline or be ready for a certain exam, but I was committed, and I would do what I needed to do. I had trouble learning how to take a blood pressure reading with a stethoscope, for instance. I didn't know exactly what I was listening for, but I borrowed blood pressure cuffs from the nursing arts lab and went around to all my fellow classmates, taking their blood pressure until I felt comfortable with what I was hearing.

My hard work paid off. For the first time in my life, I made A's and B's, and I could see that good grades were not beyond my reach. I let go of being ashamed that it took so long for me to learn.

It was demanding, but nursing school was demanding for everybody, even the fast learners. About a fifth of our class dropped out before we received our caps at six months. "Capping," as the ceremony is called, means you're ready to start working with patients under the supervision of the nursing instructor. My parents came up for my capping in October, and the class sang "The Impossible Dream" from *Man of La Mancha*, which had come out that year. After the ceremony, my parents and I went out to dinner. I had looked forward to it. I was certain that finally my parents would be pleased with what I'd accomplished, and I was especially happy about my grades. Poor grades, as far as I could tell, were the reason my parents had not liked me all through my school years. I had struggled. Since kindergarten I had not properly done my family job to get good grades. My parents needed to employ a tutor. I heard continually the background echo of *what's the matter with Sarah?* But no more. I had worked hard and given them something to be proud of.

At dinner my mother said something about how the ceremony was nice. There was talk about my father's work and some family news. Mostly we sat in awkward silence. At different times, I saw both my parents glance at their watches, and I knew they were thinking about the drive back to Meriden, calculating how long they needed to stay to fulfill their parental obligation. My parents weren't pleased with me after all. Let alone proud. Would they ever be? My parents would always be impossible puzzles I could never solve. Afterwards I returned alone to the dorm, where my friends and their extended families were still celebrating the happy day.

Back in the hospital, I found working with patients to be satisfying. After capping we were entered into clinical rotations. I enjoyed looking at the patients' charts, reading about their histories, considering the tentative diagnoses, tests, treatments, and medications. As with the class work, the patient work took me longer to complete than it would take other students, and, in my evaluations, the instructors often commented on my poor organizational skills. Still, they noted that I was knowledgeable and gave good care.

One day, early on, I was assigned a particular patient and I examined her and checked her chart, gleaning what I could. Later that morning, I stopped in to see her again and noticed she was bluish in color and unresponsive. I immediately started CPR. The woman responded, and a staff nurse then took over. It was deeply gratifying to save someone's life. The woman's name was Rose, and she was in her sixties. When I returned to the floor the following week, she asked for me and thanked me and gave me a dollar. I tried to decline, but she insisted.

We worked different shifts at the hospital, and, for a time, I worked the 11:00 p.m. to 7:00 a.m. shift. I had trouble staying awake in the wee hours of the morning, and then I found I couldn't sleep when I'd get back to my room. I found it stressful and would get sick to my stomach. Soon we were doing specialty rotations for three months each. My first was in obstetrics, and I did it during the night shift.

I cared one night for a woman who had experienced a stillbirth at delivery and then had to undergo a hysterectomy. I stayed with her all night, still wondering, when the sun finally rose the next morning and shone into her room, why such misfortune had to happen to anybody. But I also saw babies being born, a miraculous sight.

My next rotation was psychiatry. Albany Medical Center had two inpatient floors. By then I had been a nursing student for a year and three months. I was used to reading charts of people with physical problems. These patients were often young people in their twenties and thirties who had healthy bodies. They didn't look sick. I felt a bit lost, afraid of saying something inappropriate to a patient. Patients on the psychiatric floors could become easily agitated. Some were in seclusion and restrained. There was one room where everybody wore straight-jackets and they walked in circles, yelling and swearing and spitting. Elsewhere, people were on suicide watches. Some patients had eating disorders and were on feeding tubes, which they would frequently pull out. Then they'd have to be restrained so the tubes could be put back in. There was electroshock therapy. Anti-psychotic drugs were just starting to be developed at the time, Thorazine being the primary one. One day we visited a state mental institution for a day and it was even worse than our own psychiatric ward. Years later I would see *One Flew Over the Cuckoo's Nest*, a film about a mental hospital set roughly in that time period, and I was taken by how accurate it was.

It was all incredibly depressing and I felt my anxiety rising with each passing day. On patient charts I would read about ongoing read-missions and continuing psychiatric treatments, and I came to realize that many of the patients were stuck in a revolving door: admission, treatment, discharge, readmission. Making me more anxious still was reading the family histories of these patients. Many read like my own.

In our related classroom work, we studied Freud. We learned about the oedipal complex—boys who feared castration and were in competition with their fathers for the attention and love of their mothers, and girls with penis envy who were in competition with their mothers and wanted to sleep with their fathers. The literature confirmed for me that what had happened with my father was, indeed, my fault. Apparently I really did want it. I really did make him do it. The Freudian material ended up being a large part of the final exam.

I lost forty pounds working in the psych ward. I'd push food around my plate, unable to bring myself to eat it. I couldn't sleep. Some days I'd call in sick with nausea. Little by little, I began to see myself in the patients. Little by little, I began to view my future, a future of straightjackets and isolation rooms and restraints. I had read some of the attempted suicide accounts. When I had earlier worked on the surgical floor, I took care of a patient who had shot himself in the neck. His neck was mutilated and he couldn't eat or speak. He had a feeding tube and a hole in his throat to breathe. It was heartbreaking and I decided that if I ever tried to kill myself, I'd be certain to do it in such a way that my death would be assured.

Eventually, the suicidal thoughts became more frequent. The psychiatric ward of Albany Medical Center made me realize that life, in fact, was not going to be like the summer camps. Life was hopeless, mine especially so. No one loved me; no one ever would. Nobody would care if I died. I had my friends, but surely if they knew my true self, the shame and sinfulness I carried with me, they'd be repulsed and I would be justifiably shunned. I didn't even have any hatred or anger for my father that I could cling to: I'd forgiven him. Right to his face. Besides, Freud said it was my fault. In the end, I decided I didn't deserve a life of love. And I sure didn't want the life of hell I was living. It seemed only a matter of time before I'd end up in the psych ward, this time as a patient. I was still tired of living, even more so than before. The difference now was that I was no longer scared of dying.

CHAPTER 8

UNLOVED

My anxiety was getting worse and the world felt as if it was closing in on me. Nothing felt safe. My fears became my reality. I became terrified of walking down the street, believing I'd be shot by a stranger strolling past, or perhaps from somebody in a passing car. I stopped going out for short errands and I stopped going out with my friends, making excuses for why I could not go shopping or to the movies with them. I couldn't stand the thought of them getting hurt by a bullet that was meant for me. Why should they be injured or even killed when I was the one who deserved to be shot? Soon I was missing my classes in psychiatric care, and I could no longer report for duty to the psychiatric clinical area—instead I'd call into the infirmary complaining of stomach aches and nausea.

I mostly stayed in my dorm room, often sitting on my bed under the top sheet, making a tent for myself where I couldn't see the world. This was a helpful escape since, at night, I couldn't sleep or would often awake from nightmares.

After a year, I moved into a new dormitory with a larger room and a roommate. One day my roommate walked in and wondered what I was doing under my sheet. I tried to make a joke. "Just sitting under my sheet tent," I said. Later, she told my other friends, and that afternoon they all came into my room expressing their concern. Hiding out under the sheet was only one thing. They mentioned that I'd been acting inappropriately at other times, too. They knew I wasn't leaving the dorm, and that I'd been calling in sick. I hadn't been going out with them, either. They'd noticed my weight loss, too.

I assured them I was fine, but when they left I realized I'd need to move things along faster now. Before serious intervention. Before they'd have me in a straitjacket in the state mental institute.

The very next thing I remember, I was standing at the window of the room, seven stories up. I opened the window and looked down at the paved parking lot. It was a sunny day in late July, and the sun was gleaming off the cars. Seven stories seemed enough. It was a nine-story building, but I didn't have access to any of the rooms on the ninth floor. No matter. Seven would do it. All I needed to do was lean over. Gravity would do the rest.

I was ready.

And then I heard a kind, determined whisper coming from somewhere inside of me.

No, it said. *No*.

When my roommate came back into the room, she asked how I was doing and I confessed that I'd been at the window, wanting to jump. She walked me to my psychiatric instructor's office and explained to him what had happened.

Surprisingly to me, he was kind and understanding. He called the front office and had the school director call my parents, and then he stayed with me until they arrived. It took them two hours to get there, and I was never left alone in that time. While we waited, my instructor made an appointment for me with a psychiatrist in Albany. He then told me how important it was, to get the most out of psychiatric therapy, for me to be as honest as I could be.

When my parents arrived, the three of us drove to the psychiatrist's office. This was my first experience talking with a psychiatrist, and I found it intimidating. He first interviewed me privately, and I told him about wanting to jump out of the window. "Why?" he asked. I remembered my psychiatric instructor's advice to be honest, and so I told him about the sex with my father. How guilty and sinful I felt. How I deserved to die and had just wanted to get it over with.

The psychiatrist was the first person I'd ever told about having sex with my father.

He considered my disclosure for a second and then said, "Did you like it?"

I was left speechless, overwhelmed with chest pains, barely able to catch my breath. It was a feeling not unlike what I'd felt on those Sunday mornings seated beside my father at church, the physical feeling of fishhooks tearing my heart apart. I wished I was dead. I wished I had jumped.

The psychiatrist called my parents into his office and told them I needed to be hospitalized for depression. He said nothing about what I had told him. Since we lived in Connecticut, he was recommending the Institute of Living in Hartford, a private sanitarium.

My father then spoke. "My father does not get along with people," he said. "I do not get along with people. Sarah does not get along with people. So what? If she wants to kill herself, I will do nothing to stop her."

I felt numb and dizzy. The chest pains returned. This was followed by a long, uncomfortable silence. My mother, sitting next to my father, said nothing. The evidence was now conclusive. I was unloved and there was nobody who cared if I lived or died.

We drove back to Meriden, the three of us. It was a silent, awkward, endless drive.

Because I was nineteen and under age, my father's decision not to have me hospitalized was incontestable. He would acquiesce only to outpatient psychotherapy. My mother resolved to find a therapist but looked no further than her bridge club. The husband of one of the other members happened to be a psychiatrist. After my initial evaluation, Dr. McLoughlin put me on Thorazine. Eventually I'd be put on one-hundred milligrams, four times a day. I was also prescribed sleeping medication.

Meanwhile, I hated living back home, hated being in our house and being in my bedroom. I desperately wanted to return to nursing school. That fall I went back, but I lasted only a month. My anxiety remained overwhelming. I couldn't concentrate; I couldn't eat; I couldn't sleep without nightmares. For a second and final time, I left the Albany Medical Center School of Nursing. I was a failure again. Or, more accurately, I was still a failure. I lived in my bedroom praying at nights that I would not awaken, praying that God would kill me.

I continued seeing Dr. McLoughlin. Our sessions were mostly him asking how I was doing and then waiting for a response while I sat in silence. In spite of my ongoing anxiety, Dr. McLoughlin's office was comfortable enough. He was a nice man. He was my father's age, forty-one, but he had snow white hair. It turned out he and I had the same birthday. "I'm glad something good happened on that day," I told him. Thankfully, he had me sitting in a chair rather than a couch which I had initially feared because of the vulnerability the couch would have exposed me to. It was a tall, dark green leather chair that came up above my head and made me feel secure. But I still couldn't open up to Dr. McLoughlin. I was too afraid of his judgment and condemnation. What if he asked me if I liked it? I only told him I wanted to die. A scenario often played out in my mind where I took a large knife and stabbed myself in the belly, committing hari-kari in his office, blood everywhere, all over my hands, all over my legs, all over the carpet. I wanted and deserved to die. I kept the scenario to myself.

I continued to maintain my silence for the most part and one day Dr. McLoughlin said he was terminating our sessions. He said he was not the right therapist for me. I was stunned. I felt rejected again. I begged him not to stop seeing me. I offered to write letters to him. I was journaling then and it occurred to me that writing to him would be better than speaking to him, but he said that, for the therapy to work, I needed to talk to him.

"You've built a wall around yourself, Sarah," he said. "For this to work, I need you to talk to me, to share your thoughts and feelings."

"I can't talk about my dirty laundry," I said. "I'm afraid of what you'll think."

"Then I can't help you."

I took a deep breath and told him. I wanted to get it all out quickly, so, as succinctly as I could put it, I told Dr. McLoughlin about the sex. I told him I had stopped it but felt alone, guilty, ashamed, and sinful. I told him I'd been scared to tell him because I knew all about Freud and the oedipal complex and how little girls are in competition with their mothers and have penis envy and want to have sex with their fathers.

Dr. McLoughlin listened and explained that his take on the oedipal complex was that children learn their roles from their parents, how to be men and women, nothing as sordid as what I'd come to believe. He said that Freud's biggest contribution was the idea that many of our behaviors are done unconsciously. Often, we're not aware of why we do what we do. Psychotherapy, he explained, is a way to discover our motivations and help change our behaviors, especially negative ones.

He didn't ask me any more about the sex with my father, sensing that I was like a frightened deer, ready to bolt if he pried any further. Most importantly, he never asked me if I liked it. It struck me then that he genuinely wanted me to feel better. The idea that he wanted to terminate our sessions because he was not the right therapist for me came from a sincere place and a sign to me that Dr. McLoughlin was looking out for my welfare. For my part, I felt in some sense that I'd been heard and accepted. I could feel my body releasing some deeply held fears and a small seed of trust was planted. I continued to see Dr. McLoughlin. In all the years of therapy I would have with him, we never spoke about the abuse again.

In the meantime, I took a job working at a seventy-bed nursing home. I had to get a job. I could not live at home and not have one. The importance of work was always stressed in our family and it was unthinkable that anyone physically healthy would stay home and not work.

Working at the nursing home made me realize I didn't have the market cornered on suffering. I took care of patients who had strokes, who could not speak, who were paralyzed on one side, who could not walk or write or read. Some could barely eat baby food without choking. I took care of patients with dementia who kept asking me for directions to their homes, or kept asking for help but were unable to explain what help they needed.

I cared for one woman who was young by nursing home standards. She was only in her sixties, but she had a spastic palsy that made her arms and legs move uncontrollably in uncoordinated, jerky motions. She had to be fed. She was incontinent and she could not walk or sit in a chair. She went from her bed to a padded recliner and in the recliner she had to be in a chest restraint to keep her from falling out. It was hard to understand her slurred speech, but her mind was clear. She'd always greet the staff members with a smile and she always said please and thank you. She was grateful for anything that we did for her. She loved classical music and she had her radio station tuned to the classical music station. She needed the volume set high and anytime we cared for her we had to turn it down to better hear her slurred speech. Then we had to remember to turn the volume up on our way out.

She spoke about her daughter and her grandchildren, whose photos were updated regularly on her bureau. She seemed content and was kind to others in her suffering. I was astonished by her grace and dignity. Why was she so cheerful? She had every excuse to be angry and bitter and depressed. How could she be so grateful? There I was with a young, healthy, working body. Maybe, it began to occur to me that I needed to be more grateful, too.

I became especially close to a resident named Nellie. Nellie was in her late 70s, frail and petite, but with bright blue eyes and an easy smile. She had gray hair that she wore in braids with ribbons and she seemed like a sweet, overgrown, gray-haired Raggedy Ann doll. She liked to hug everyone and I enjoyed receiving her hugs and hugging her back. Besides Nellie, I had nobody in my everyday life to share a hug with. We enjoyed each other's company and made each other laugh. I would buy her little things: chocolates and cards. One Easter I made tiny Easter baskets in small medicine cups with cellophane, grass, and jelly beans, sugar-free ones for the diabetic patients. I gave each patient a basket, but Nellie seemed to appreciate hers the most.

I kept seeing Dr. McLoughlin, but eventually my father sent him a letter declaring he would no longer be responsible for the doctor's bill. Dr. McLoughlin showed me the letter. The sessions were twice a week at twenty-five dollars per session and my medication was ten dollars a week. My take-home pay from the nursing home was sixty dollars a week. There would be nothing left, and there was still cab fare to and from the sessions. But I told Dr. McLoughlin that I would be responsible for his bill.

"My concern," he said, "is that your father wants to terminate our therapy." This was a real concern. Since I was underage and the sexual abuse was not happening at this time, my father could have done so without consequence. I told Dr. McLoughlin, that no, my father's interest was only the money. I began working overtime and weekends for extra income. I worked Sundays, no longer going to church. For my father's part, he tried another tack to stop the therapy, offering to buy me a new car if I "would just snap out of it." I stared at him blankly. A car made financial sense to my father. Therapy did not. My behavior—seeing Dr. McLoughlin—was just so much adolescent drama.

I couldn't have done much with a car even if I had accepted his offer, which I could never have done. I still hadn't learned to drive and with my anxiety and inability to focus, I couldn't have passed a driver's test anyway. In fact, my father had been driving me to the nursing home every morning on his way to work. It was a five-mile commute and I hated riding with him. I huddled like a frightened animal against the passenger side door with my hand on the door handle, ready and willing to open it and dive out while the car was in motion if I felt as though I would need to. I wondered sometimes if it would kill me to jump out of the car, but decided that we probably never went fast enough on the local roads that led to the nursing home.

I worked from seven in the morning until three-thirty in the afternoon, and, in good weather, I would walk home. The road from the nursing home was bordered by a golf course and a pond and pasture land. I enjoyed walking home, looking at the trees and the flowers and the birds. I enjoyed the changing seasons. I noticed my anxiety receding as I walked. After a few months, I realized I had stopped thinking about getting shot by a passerby. Only if it was pouring rain or there was a snowstorm would I ask a staff member to give me a ride, and then hope to not have to hear about how beautiful my house was or how the neighborhood was so exclusive. Even if nothing was said, I could often see the thoughts in their expressions. I felt guilty and embarrassed. I didn't deserve to live there.

After work on Mondays and Thursdays, I would take a cab to Dr. McLoughlin's office, which was in town, ten miles away. I'd take the bus back home, walking the final mile from the bus stop to our house. My father was always at work and my mother never offered to pick me up. One afternoon, the cab driver was late, making me late for my appointment, and I refused to pay him. He chased me, yelling, "Police! Police!" Eventually he chased me into Dr. McLoughlin's waiting room. Dr. McLoughlin came out to see what the commotion was and ended up paying the cab driver. I walked into his office afterwards and explained my justifiable outrage. That led, in subsequent sessions, to working on my basic social skills. With my history, I was not schooled well in dealing with others. Dr. McLoughlin helped me to communicate better. I was laboring under the assumption that people should know what I'm thinking. And I was always worried about what others thought of me. "Don't worry about what other people think of you," Dr. McLoughlin advised. "Concern yourself about what you think of others and how you treat them." We talked about disagreements I might have with fellow workers and how to handle them. Dr. McLoughlin taught me rudimentary social skills, the kind most people learn at home from their mothers and fathers.

I saw nothing but suffering in the world. My own suffering was intolerable and dying seemed the only option. I told Dr. McLoughlin that if I was in control of the nuclear button, I would blow up the world and put it and me out of our misery. Emblematic of this thinking was a patient at the nursing home who refused to eat, essentially starving herself. She wanted to die and I thought about how easy it would be to help her end her misery. The narcotics and medications were locked, but the needles and syringes were available and the insulin was kept in an unsecured refrigerator. I could fill a syringe with insulin and give her a simple injection. The woman would go into diabetic shock and die and no one would be the wiser. Dr. McLoughlin said that, as medical people, our duty is to first do no harm. Secondly, we don't have the right to impose our moral views on others, even when, as in this case, our views might coincide with theirs.

One afternoon, months into my therapy, we talked about my feelings of being unloved. This, I explained, was what had led to my thoughts of suicide. I was unloved and, worse, certain that I would remain so. How could anybody who knew me, really knew me, knew my secrets and my shame, ever find me worthy of love? I was destined to a life of isolation and contempt. Surely I deserved no more than this.

Dr. McLoughlin looked thoughtful and then said, "You know, Sarah, if you were my daughter, I would love you. I would certainly love you as a daughter." He was looking me directly in the eye and I knew he was being sincere.

After a long silence, I quietly replied, "Really?"

"Yes, I really could love you as a daughter." And then to make certain there were no misinterpretations, he added, "But only as a daughter."

Dr. McLoughlin knew about love for a daughter. He had a daughter named LeeAnn, who was in my sister's class in high school. In some alternate universe, I could be loved as LeeAnn was loved. This was hard to absorb. For several moments, I could say nothing. And then I felt tears rolling down my cheeks.

CHAPTER 9

THERAPY

The wall of shame and loneliness had been breached. I cried all the way home. On the bus, a lady came over to me and asked me if I was okay. I managed a smile and waved her away. It was astonishing to me that someone who knew about my horrible secret, who knew about my ignorance and sin and shame and guilt, could find me loveable. I felt that a salve had been applied to my wounded heart. I was touched by a mixture of joy, gratitude, and amazement. Dr. McLoughlin said that he could love me as a daughter and deep inside I would hold onto those words. Someone now cared if I lived or died.

My therapy with Dr. McLoughlin continued. Most of it revolved around understanding day-to-day social interactions. If a staff member at the nursing home frowned while looking in my direction, I would become anxious and upset. What had I said? What had I done? It never occurred to me that my fellow employee might have been having a bad day, that the frown might have nothing to do with me, that maybe the most appropriate reaction would be to take an interest and ask how they were doing. Dr. McLoughlin helped me see that. He also helped me see that someone could disagree with me and still like me, a foreign concept to me up until then.

Therapy was good for me and so was work. I needed to work, of course, to pay Dr. McLoughlin and to pay for my medication. But I was glad for it. I figured if I was going to be miserable, I might as well be miserable at work as home. At least at work I could help people. It felt good knowing I could make someone who was uncomfortable or sick be more comfortable or even smile.

When I first started at the nursing home, I had assumed that old people were learned and wise. But I'd soon discovered that these were people struggling with serious chronic diseases, both physical and mental. Unlike when I was a student, where I might have to interact with a patient for just a few weeks, these were people I worked with for months on end. They were doing the best they could and I came to more fully appreciate their challenges and difficulties, as much, at least, as any twenty year old could appreciate them. It made me feel useful to be there.

I began eating better and I started to put on some of the sixty pounds I'd ultimately lost. Every morning, after breakfast was served to the patients and the patients who needed to be fed were taken care of, the staff would have its breakfast in shifts. We'd go to the dining room and have oatmeal, eggs, juice, and coffee. I ate breakfast and lunch at work. At home for dinner, I'd take small portions and mostly push the food around my plate. Later I'd have snacks in my room. Sometimes I'd eat with the beech trees.

Notwithstanding the moments of satisfaction at work, my general anxiety was not abating. I still felt chest pains, the fishhooks tearing at my heart. It would be hard to breathe at times. I still had feelings of hyper alertness, fear that something terrible could happen at any moment. Life itself seemed frightening. Things that others seemed to grasp so easily often seemed impossible for me to understand. Despite Dr. McLoughlin's direction, I still misunderstood what others might say to me or misinterpret their behaviors toward me. I felt ignorant and vulnerable. Sometimes at work I'd become overwhelmed and I'd have to rest in a patient's room, sitting down in the visitor's chair. Then I'd have to consciously think about what I needed to do next, how to move forward with my day.

During one therapy session, I told Dr. McLoughlin I was always afraid. "Sarah," he asked me, "where is your courage?" I didn't have an answer. Dr. McLoughlin told me that everybody has fears. This was something I did not know. I assumed most people had their lives together, that their lives were always on track. Dr. McLoughlin explained that it wasn't helpful to dwell on that which I had little or no control over.

Over time, we talked about how I was constantly afraid of making mistakes and the consequences of them. Every mistake seemed deadly to me and I was paralyzed by fear. Dr. McLoughlin would tell me that everybody makes mistakes and that the thing is to learn what causes them so that you don't make them again. "But I don't like making mistakes," I would say. Mistakes are how we learn, he'd counter. It's important to take chances, he would say, and to be mindful of what the worst thing would be that could happen. The consequences are usually never as serious as what we might believe. And then you can step back, evaluate, and learn. Then make new decisions as needed. Most mistakes can be rectified, Dr. McLoughlin insisted. Eventually, I began thinking of the courage in the heroes of the musicals and movies I liked, and I decided I would try to work on finding my own courage, to try to act courageous like those characters who, like me, had challenges they were trying to overcome.

At most sessions with Dr. McLoughlin, I would tell him how unhappy I was. "Sarah," he said to me one day, "you are responsible for your own happiness." This infuriated me. It was unfair. Dr. McLoughlin, of all people, knew my story. How could I be happy with my life? And why would it be *my* responsibility to be so? How could it possibly be up to me to make myself happy considering everything I had been through and everything I was struggling with?

"*I* am responsible for *my* happiness?!" I shouted at him. I went on a tirade about my life. By then, I was no longer reticent in front of Dr. McLoughlin. The thoughts of hari-kari had subsided and I was more willing to be vulnerable and open with him, even in anger. "Somebody needs to fix my life!" I continued. "Not me. I have enough problems. I need to be taken care of. I need to be loved!" It was mind-boggling to me that Dr. McLoughlin couldn't seem to grasp this. Hadn't he heard anything I'd been saying?

He quietly and respectfully listened to me rant and said, "Sarah, no one else knows what will make you happy. You have to discover that for yourself. We all have to discover what makes us happy and then we need to take those actions that will help create that happiness."

"But my parents should be responsible for my happiness. Maybe a boyfriend someday. As my therapist, you should be responsible!"

"No, Sarah. Not your parents. Not me. And not anybody else. Just you. And then, when you are happy, you can share that happiness with others. And they can share their happiness with you. But they're not responsible for your happiness and you're not responsible for theirs."

Over time, we discussed what made me happy. This became the core of my therapy with Dr. McLoughlin for months and months. I talked about wanting to be a registered nurse—to help people, to make a difference for them. We focused on the steps I needed to take to be readmitted to nursing school, but I felt overwhelmed by the process, and I thought, too, of my psychiatric history as being one more barrier. I was sure I'd be turned down. "I'll bet I won't get in," I said.

"Don't ever bet against yourself, Sarah," Dr. McLoughlin said. "You never know what good things can happen in life. Betting against yourself doesn't get you anywhere. You have to pull for yourself. Everybody does." I tried to pin him down on what good things might happen to me, but he refused to be specific. "Being positive and working toward a hopeful future," he said, "will allow you to recognize and enjoy good things when they come your way." The idea of something good coming my way had not occurred to me. I thought of good things in the past, like summer camps or trips to Asheville, but these things seemed so very long ago.

I kept seeing Dr. McLoughlin twice a week. My medication was slowly decreased and eventually I was switched to Librium. I was more even-keeled and I took Dr. McLoughlin's advice and applied myself to the steps necessary to get back to nursing school and in September of 1968, I was admitted as a transfer student to Waterbury Hospital School of Nursing, a forty-minute drive away. This would enable me to continue seeing Dr. McLoughlin whom by then I was referring to more informally as Dr. Mac.

Before I left for school, and much to my surprise, my father announced he would buy me a new car. We went to the Ford dealership and my father specified a budget. The Mustang I wanted was out of reach, but I was happy with my second choice—a 1969 cranberry red, four-door Falcon hardtop with a black interior and bench seats. I finally took a driving class and got my license and was soon driving.

Before going to Waterbury, I ended my work at the nursing home. I didn't say goodbye to any of the patients, assuming most would not miss me. I didn't even say goodbye to Nellie, the resident I had become closest to, the one who gave me hugs. A couple of weeks later, I went in to collect my last paycheck and the people in the office told me Nellie had kept asking for me. It would be decades before I would come to understand that, by not dealing with my own pain by saying goodbye to Nellie, I had essentially abandoned her. I've felt ashamed ever since to think of how I'd hurt this woman whom I had cared for so much. I learned from this mistake to always say goodbye—even if it's painful.

At nursing school, as a transfer student, it was hard to make friends. Many friendships had already been formed between the other students going back to their freshman years, but it helped that I had a car. I often got invited along for outings for that reason, but that was good enough for me. Meanwhile, I maintained a part-time job in the hospital on the weekends. Aunt Lillian took care of tuition but, without any financial help from my parents, I needed to fund my expenses for everything else.

I graduated from nursing school in May of 1970. I received a red rose and my diploma, and I proudly wore the white uniform, white stockings, and white cap with the black stripe. There was no celebration on the part of my family, but by then I had learned not to expect one.

And, by then, my parents had split up. I'd been there at the break-up's inception. A year earlier, back in Meriden, I was out with my parents, sitting in the backseat of my father's Chrysler. I have no recollection of where we were going or coming from. My parents were talking in the front seat, but I wasn't paying attention. I was looking out the window, watching the trees and telephone poles go by, lost in my own thoughts. But I heard my father say something in reply to some question or statement by my mother and his reply staggered me. I'll never know what my mother said to him, but I remember his answer clearly: "Well, yes, I *was* a little fresh with Sarah and I petted her a little." I also clearly remember my mother's response: "Then I need a divorce."

The two spoke as if I was not present. Not long after that, my mother would move out. I knew that the admission my father made was the excuse for which my mother had been looking for quite some time. Lacking the courage to leave of her own accord for her own reasons, she now had an out. As to what exactly my father had done to me and what he'd meant by "petting," she never took the time to ask me.

CHAPTER 10

ROLE MODELS

My mother's silence on my father's abuse was deafening. Such was my level of need, however, that when she finally moved out of our house and into an apartment of her own and asked if I'd like to live with her, I considered the idea. I didn't want her to be lonely. And I still wanted a relationship with my mother.

Before the apartment, my mother had actually moved into Lillian's home for a few months. Despite being on my father's side of the family, Lillian had spent enough time with my mother's side to maintain a position of neutrality where the marriage was concerned. She'd come along with us a few times on our visits to see Aunt Iris and Grandmother, and she had found kindred spirits there. Their Southern refinement had matched up well with her New England sophistication.

Brenda was home from the University of Connecticut for the summer when my mother packed a suitcase and drove away in the Chrysler. Not wanting to spend the summer alone with our father in Meriden, she came up to Waterbury, and I got her a room on my dorm floor.

After the summer, my mother returned to Meriden to resume the elementary school teaching job she'd found after I had graduated from high school, after she'd received her degree from Central Connecticut State University. It seems clear in retrospect that she obtained her degree because she'd known for some time that she would eventually leave my father. When she started teaching, it was at my old elementary school—remedial reading, the exact thing I had needed when I was a little girl attending that school. That's when she took the apartment.

Dr. Mac rarely gave me advice in direct terms, choosing instead to suggest things to me in questions that I'd be forced to think through, but when I told him I was thinking of moving in with my mother, he dropped any pretense of subtlety. "Sarah," he said, "do not move in with your mother. That would *not* be good for you."

I stayed at Waterbury and, in the fall, I took the boards, two days of written exams that I studied desperately hard for. I was still convinced I was stupid. For every hour the "normal" student would have to study, I assumed I'd have to study two. But I passed. I was now a licensed RN.

In the meantime, improbably, I endeavored to keep in touch with my father. I was intent on being forgiving, as my Christian faith taught me. I was also trying to regard myself as an adult and believed I could interact with my father on an adult level. One time I got us tickets to see *Man of La Mancha*. Of course I had sung "The Impossible Dream" with my nursing school class during our capping ceremony, but I had no idea the storyline revolved around a prostitute. The production included a rape scene. The evening with my father was long and exceedingly uncomfortable, full of anxiety. When the show was over, I left immediately for Waterbury.

Before long, there was a cutback in staffing at Waterbury Hospital and I took a position at St. Mary's, the other major hospital in the town. I left the dorm and rented a room in a house from a kind elderly couple where I lived for eight months before finding my own small apartment. At St. Mary's, it seemed to be quite a big deal that I lived alone, a single girl with her own apartment. The rest of the nurses on the staff were either single and still living with their parents, engaged and planning their weddings (and still living with their parents), or married and living with their husbands and/or children. That was the natural progression for women in those days. A few years later, *The Mary Tyler Moore Show* would glamorize the life of a single woman out on her own, but it wasn't looked at glamorously in Waterbury in 1970.

Despite my continued therapy with Dr. Mac, I still found myself struggling. I'd never lost my anxieties and the job at St. Mary's was making them worse. Miss McGinty was the head nurse. She was in her fifties, a short, thin woman with close-cropped gray hair, a stern face, and no makeup. She was unmarried, although there were rumors she'd been going out with a Jewish doctor for twenty-five years; her being an Irish Catholic had made marriage impossible. Miss McGinty was no-nonsense. Humorless. A witch. "How's the boss riding her broom today?" we nurses would joke in the smoke-filled break room.

Miss McGinty held the key to the narcotics and you had to go to her and ask for it to get the prescribed medication for your patient. She would constantly make negative remarks about the patients, questioning their need for this or that drug, regardless of the fact that the patient might be in need and regardless of the fact that the medication had been doctor-ordered. I wasn't good at masking my emotions and Miss McGinty could see at a glance my anxiety whenever she would hesitate to give me the key, handing it over to me slowly and deliberately. "Well, don't get all spastic, Miss Snell," she would say. I never knew exactly what she meant by that, but I found it hurtful, nonetheless.

Witch or not, I still wanted to please. My level of self-esteem required it. One of the other nurses took to calling me "Beagle" because I wanted to please everybody "like a beagle dog," as she explained it to the rest of the staff. Everyone laughed and I smiled, desperate to fit in, consciously unaware that I was proving her point.

Seemingly everyone smoked in the hospital. It was the times. There was some general knowledge that smoking was not good for you, but nobody seemed to recognize just how bad it was. People smoked everywhere: hospitals, office buildings, airplanes, restaurants. Dr. McLoughlin smoked during our sessions. In the hospital, doctors, nurses, and patients alike smoked. When I took vacations to North Carolina, people would give me orders for cartons of cigarettes, which weren't taxed there the way they were taxed in Connecticut. I dutifully obliged, stuffing the cartons into my suitcase.

The doctors, of course, were all men back then, another function of the times. Protocol demanded the utmost respect toward them. Nurses were considered the doctors' handmaidens. When a doctor came into your nurse's station, you stood and offered him your chair.

Outside of work, my life was better. I had a social life. I had been dating since nursing school, although never seriously with anybody, and I still had friends from school, too. Over time, I became best friends with a girl named Amanda, who had been a foster child. Amanda had a boyfriend who was several years older than she was. George was a high school dropout but had become involved with his family's business and made good money. He drove a 1967 red convertible Mustang with a stick shift, black leather bucket seats, dual exhaust, and fancy chrome wheels. Sometimes Amanda would get the car and we would drive around with the top down. She'd rev the engine at stoplights and we both felt cool and hip. I was starting to feel young.

But Amanda didn't get along with George's family and the two argued a lot. After one particularly bad fight, Amanda asked me if she should break up with George. I've since learned this is a dangerous question to navigate. Your answer can come back to haunt you. I told her yes; I thought she deserved better than George. Ultimately, she reconnected with George, they married, and they had a baby.

Still, regardless of knowing how I felt about her husband, Amanda seemed to value my friendship, and even asked me to babysit for her one night. She and George went out and I watched over their three-month-old little girl. Not long after the two had left the house, the baby began to cry and then scream. I held her, fed her, walked her around the house, rocked her. Nothing helped. Her screaming went on relentlessly until I finally snapped. I put the baby in her crib and screamed back at her. *"Shut up! Shut up! Shut up! Shut up!"* Then I stormed out of her bedroom. The baby was fine when Amanda and George returned later.

I never babysat for Amanda again, always making excuses whenever she would ask. I was ashamed. I was a licensed RN, and yet I lost my patience and screamed irrationally at a baby. There was no justification. I knew enough not to have shaken the baby, but it scared me to think that, without my education, I might have done so. My excuse-making to Amanda and the feelings of shame I felt caused our friendship to wither and eventually die.

Back at St. Mary's Hospital, things were becoming worse. Due to staffing problems, I was relegated to a day-night rotating shift. Two weeks day shift, one-week night shift. This was before research revealed how counterproductive such a schedule is. I did not handle it well. I slept poorly. I'd get home at seven-thirty or eight in the morning and try to sleep, but I never made it past ten-thirty or eleven. I'd try to nap in the afternoon, but with limited success. I was tired all the time. At eleven at night, when my body was crying for sleep, I'd have to report for duty. I'd be exhausted during my shift, yet I knew I had to be responsible for thirty patients. I ate poorly—snacks and fast foods and unhealthy breakfasts. I drank coffee constantly. My anxiety became worse. By three or four in the morning, I was vomiting bile in the bathroom.

I started losing weight again and I developed stomach problems and became anemic. Eventually I was diagnosed with a duodenal ulcer. The slow blood loss from the ulcer was responsible for my anemia and I imagined bleeding to death internally, an actual possibility. I was terrified. Once again, I gave myself to Christ. I became involved with an Episcopal church. To me, it had the best elements of both Protestantism and Catholicism. It had the beautiful music that I'd loved from the Protestant services I'd attended since childhood, but it also had Catholic rituals, like Communion at every service. The church operated on the liturgical calendar, too, and I enjoyed the different seasons—Advent, Christmastide, Epiphany, Lent, Easter, Ascension, and Pentecost. The homily for one of the services asked this question: what would you do if you knew you only had six months to live? It was meant to help one bring into focus those things in a person's life that are most important. With my duodenal ulcer, I felt as if it was directed toward me.

I began thinking hard about my mortality. I had just been surviving day to day, but now I started thinking about getting myself well and what my priorities were. The recommended treatment for the ulcer at the time was hospitalization, medication, and a bland diet. I elected to take a break instead. I knew that if I had that hypothetical six months to live, one thing I'd do would be to go to Asheville. I hadn't visited Aunt Iris's in three years, and, besides, I knew that rest and relaxation at Aunt Iris's home would be better than any hospital stay. She and my grandmother were thrilled to see me. I took my own prescribed medications and Aunt Iris was only too happy to accommodate my bland dietary needs.

I stayed at Aunt Iris's for two weeks. At one point, I was reintroduced to a cousin. Casey Lynn was fifteen years older than me, tall and blonde. A successful single woman, Casey Lynn was a guidance counselor at a community college in Asheville. She was an only child and her parents had both died when she was in her early thirties. She lived in her family's three-bedroom house, which she shared with her aunt Jenny Sue. Aunt Iris had Casey Lynn and Jenny Sue over for dinner a couple of times while I was visiting and Casey Lynn and I enjoyed each other's company. She was smart. She had a master's degree and was a hardworking, accomplished woman. When I returned to Waterbury, Casey Lynn and I kept in touch, often phoning and writing letters. We exchanged Christmas and birthday gifts. One time, Casey Lynn said she'd always wanted to visit Maine and so we planned a tentative vacation together for the following summer.

Back in Waterbury, my ulcer had improved, but it still scared me. I decided I could no longer work the day-night rotating shift; I needed a guaranteed day shift. But the hospital wouldn't accommodate my request. I quit and, shortly afterwards, accepted a position at a nursing home close to my apartment, taking a pay cut in the process.

I was still seeing Dr. Mac, once a week and sometimes twice. He was still talking to me about being responsible for my own happiness and my interactions with others. He observed that I had unreasonable expectations of people. I was needy. If somebody didn't live up to some manufactured idea I had about their treatment toward me, I would be hurt. I unreasonably asked more from others than what they could give me. But, even as he told me this, I found it confusing and hard to follow. I sensed Dr. Mac was telling me something important about myself, but it wasn't fully registering. I didn't know any other way to be. I had no frame of reference for change.

But I worked on taking Dr. Mac's advice. It was a gradual process. I wanted to at least try to take charge of my own happiness, as he had advised, as well as work on my interactions with others, but it was slow going. That Thanksgiving, in an attempt at self-improvement, and rather than spend the holiday alone, I asked our parish priest if he knew of an elderly person who might not have a place to go for the holiday. He introduced me to a sweet old lady named Miss Tuttle and I took her out to dinner, sharing the day with her instead of being lonely and miserable.

I was alone that Christmas, too. My mother and Brenda went to visit my grandmother that year. I was not asked to join them. I woke up early for work on Christmas Day and brought a radio into the hospital for the patients so they could listen to Christmas music. Afterwards, I went home and opened presents by myself. My mother had sent me some things. Dr. Mac had even sent me a present—a hot plate. My father gave me another radio. That evening, I took Miss Tuttle out to Valle's Steakhouse, which made the day a lot less lonely.

Dr. Mac enjoyed hearing about my reaching out to Miss Tuttle, and, some time afterward, knowing of my loneliness, he asked me if I would like to meet his mother in nearby Naugatuck. I said yes, and he introduced me to her, telling her I was the sister of his daughter's classmate, rather than introducing me as a patient, although I suspect she knew the truth.

Brigid McLoughlin was in her early seventies, with snow-white hair like her son's, which she wore in braids from one ear to the other, making a beautiful, white braided crown. She had rosy cheeks and bright, blue, smiling Irish eyes. She insisted I call her Brig rather than Mrs. McLoughlin. Brig lived in a charming, turn-of-the-century Victorian cottage with a wraparound porch. There were two bedrooms upstairs, but she'd converted a small downstairs den into her bedroom so she wouldn't have to traverse the stairs. The room barely held her single bed, her bureau, and a nightstand. Downstairs in the dining room, there was an antique Seth Thomas wall clock and you could hear its relentless ticking throughout the first floor. At the other end of the dining room was a large painting of sailboats on a blue-gray pallet that hung over the sideboard. The artist was her son, Dr. Mac.

It was Brig's family home. She had been an only child, born in 1900 to Irish immigrants. Naugatuck was a factory town, dominated by Goodyear Rubber, and everybody worked "in the rubber," as it was put. She'd married a protestant civil engineer. The wedding had been held in the rectory, since they couldn't be married in the Catholic Church. Among other projects, her husband worked on the George Washington Bridge, spanning the Hudson from Manhattan to Fort Lee, New Jersey. His work took them all over and they lived for a time in Des Moines, Iowa, where they owned a farm. Eventually, he was sent to Korea during the Korean War and died there in a civilian accident. Ultimately, following her husband's death, she made her way back to Naugatuck.

I began spending free time with Brig, who genuinely seemed to enjoy my company. And she enjoyed seeing just me. Previously, if I was welcomed anywhere, like at Aunt Iris's, I was welcomed along with my mother and sister. I was not familiar with being welcomed by myself. I was touched and delightfully surprised by Brig's kind gestures toward me. She didn't drive, so, on my day off, I would take her to the store for her weekly shopping. Back at her place, she'd make me lunch—typically macaroni and cheese with boiled potatoes, potatoes being the only necessary vegetable in Brig's house. Sometimes after visiting her, I'd stay overnight in one of her cozy upstairs bedrooms. We'd enjoy breakfast the next morning and drink coffee.

That Dr. Mac—that any therapist—would involve a patient with a family member was remarkable. He knew the relationship would be of benefit to both me and Brig. Yet Brig and I knew the limits. We never spoke about her son and his work. And my involvement with Brig never extended further into her family. I wasn't invited to Thanksgiving or Christmas, for instance, and I never visited when Dr. Mac and his family were visiting. Brig and I both understood the boundaries.

One late autumn day, Brig wanted me to go with her to a cloistered convent in Bethlehem, Connecticut, a town I'd never heard of before. A relative of Brig's had once been a nun in the convent. Brig had visited her, but it had been years before and she hadn't been back since. Along the way, the trees made a magnificent combination of yellows, reds, and oranges that glowed in the bright sunshine and cool fall air, creating canopies of color over the narrow, two-lane back roads of Connecticut. At the convent, we said a prayer in the chapel and visited the gift shop. These were the only places not off-limits to guests. Through a large, wrought-iron gate, Brig talked briefly to a sister in her traditional habit. Brig enjoyed the day, appreciating it in a way that youth has a tendency never to do. For Brig, there might not be another autumn. She lived each day as fully as she could. "I know it's going to be a good day," she'd tell me, "when I wake up and find my arms aren't hitting the sides of my casket." I laughed with Brig. There were few people in my life I had ever laughed with.

I kept spending time with Brig. Eventually she introduced me to her "kissing cousin," a retired RN named Mary who had coincidentally worked at St. Mary's Hospital in Waterbury. Mary lived in a small, simple house with black-framed pictures in her living room of the late Kennedys, John and Bobby. She kept her door unlocked and when we'd visit her, Brig never bothered to knock or ring the bell. She'd simply walk in and announce, "Hi, Mary, I'm here!" This always surprised me. I thought of growing up in my parents' house, where the doors were locked at all times and nobody would dream of dropping by without calling ahead. Mary would always welcome us inside for coffee and a sweet. She'd reached the age, she told us, where she knew more people in the cemetery than people who were alive, and I wondered what that felt like.

Brig never criticized me. Sometimes she'd subtly offer guidance, saying to me "so what?" when I'd take something too seriously or suggest patience when she'd see me getting angry in traffic or irritated by a long line at the store. We'd play canasta. I was sometimes not a good loser, but Brig would smile and say, "You know, Sarah, life is like a game. You just have to play the hand you're dealt." She told me once it seemed to her as if I wanted to remain single. I didn't; I wanted to meet someone and marry and have a family. After all, ever since Dr. Mac had said he could love me, it struck me as possible that someone else could, too. I could meet and fall in love with a man, something I desperately wanted. I wondered how it was that Brig had received a different impression.

One time she told me the story of having fallen in her tub years before. It was after her husband had died and she was all alone. Her leg had been broken in eight places and she couldn't get out of the tub. She laughed, telling me how, in the midst of lying there, her main concern was how she was going to look in her coffin, given that she was unable to straighten her legs. Somebody found her the next day and took her to the hospital, where she had surgery and metal plates put in her legs. Brig was in a wheelchair for three years. At one point, she was told she would never walk again, but Brig had been a physio-therapist, one of the first in the country. She worked on herself. Her therapy was exercise and a lot of massage. For the rest of her life, Brig would have a slight limp, but her patience and perseverance meant she would be able to walk.

Brig's perseverance was apparently a lifelong trait. She mentioned an aunt who'd observed, when Brig was little, that, when she fell, she always got right back up. Brig told me this as a lesson to be learned, and, more than once, hearing of some unimportant and minor setback I might have experienced, she'd say, "Sarah, so what? When you fall, you get right back up again."

In the summer of 1972, my cousin Casey Lynn and I took that Maine vacation we had talked about before. She drove up to Waterbury and then we drove throughout New England in her expensive blue Dodge with air-conditioning, power windows, white leather bucket seats, and cruise control. I couldn't stop admiring this successful, inde-pendent woman. She'd been taking flying instructions about that time, too, and she had a boyfriend.

Along the way, we searched for Walden Pond, where Henry David Thoreau had lived, but in the pre-GPS days, we never found it. Casey Lynn introduced me to poetry. We talked about Walt Whitman. We discussed religion. She helped me see the stories in the Bible in a larger context—the symbolism and the poetry, rather than the literal inter-pretations I'd been taught as a child. She introduced me to the writings of Kahlil Gibran. "And if you would know God," Gibran had written, "be not therefore a solver of riddles." This stuck with me.

Like me, Casey Lynn liked the outdoors and hiking and trees. She seemed like a kindred spirit to me and she became like an older sister, or maybe an aunt. She was only seven years younger than my mother, after all. Once, during our trip to Maine, she kissed me lightly on the cheek. It came out of the blue, but it seemed like a kiss of genuine affection, nothing more, and I gave it no further thought.

In August, I turned twenty-five. I stopped by my mother's apart-ment with twenty-five red roses to celebrate her twenty-five years as a mother, and to help cheer her up since her divorce. I knew she'd never gotten flowers from my father before. She received the roses indiffer-ently, politely saying, "Thank you" and nothing more. I still didn't know how to please her.

When Uncle Clifford died, my grandmother called my mother to tell her the news. She called our house and my father had to give her my mother's new phone number. She'd never told my grandmother she was leaving my father or getting a divorce.

After Maine, Casey Lynn and I continued to keep in touch. I would visit Asheville a couple of times a year, staying at Aunt Iris's but spending time with my cousin. It was Casey Lynn who told me about my mother's past, about her schooling at St. Genevieve-of-the-Pines, of which I had heard nothing before. Casey Lynn told me the story of my grandfather's temper, too—about the driver of the car that hit my mother and about how my grandfather had begun chasing him with a shotgun.

Casey Lynn knew that I thought I was stupid. I told her as much. "Sarah, you're smart," she'd argue. "Besides, look at how smart your parents are. Look at your sister. It's in your genes. Unless you've had a serious disease or some kind of head trauma, you have to be intelligent." I never believed her and one day she said, "I'll prove it." As a guidance counselor, Casey Lynn was also a licensed psychometrist, certified to administer intelligence tests. She had me take an IQ test and I was stunned to learn that I scored above average.

This was a turning point for me. I hadn't even expected an average score, let alone an above-average one. Being stupid, but hardworking in what I cared about, was the lens that I saw myself through. Now I began to see myself differently and I wondered what might be possible for me. I even started reading books for recreation, something I had shied away from before, thinking I was too slow to comprehend whole books or to stick with them. Dr. Mac had helped me feel as if I could be loved. Casey Lynn had helped me think I could be smart. The tectonic plates of my life were shifting.

I didn't want to work at the nursing home for the rest of my life, and, with the IQ test results, I began thinking I could go to college. By then, I could see that, eventually, nurses were going to be expected to have college degrees and I decided to find a program where I could get a bachelor's in nursing. I started researching colleges, only to learn that three years of class work would be required. This was infuriating. I was a licensed RN. Why could I not earn a degree in less time? Besides, there was the question of money. Knowing I had no financial support, knowing I could depend on nobody but myself, I'd lived frugally and managed to save much of the one-hundred dollars a week I'd been making. From 1970 to 1974, I put away five-thousand dollars, a tidy sum, but not enough for three years of college. Finally, after much searching, I came across St. Joseph's College in Standish, Maine. St. Joseph's was offering a full-time, one-year program where I could get a Bachelor of Science degree in professional arts. I was accepted to begin my classes in September of 1974.

I became emboldened. The IQ test was a big factor. So too was the church. I hadn't forgotten the homily about having six months to live. Continued therapy sessions with Dr. Mac helped, too. I was on a search for the courage within that he had talked about and one day I saw the film version of *Paint Your Wagon*. It had just come out and I was taken by the lyrics: "When will I be there? I don't know; When will I get there? I ain't certain; All that I know is I am on my way." In March of that year, I took a chance and quit the nursing home. And with nothing keeping me in Waterbury, I moved to Asheville and took the third bedroom in Casey Lynn's house. My long-range plan was to go to Maine in the fall, spend the school year there, and then return to Asheville with my degree. I didn't know what the future held, but at least now I was "on my way." Perhaps in Asheville I could meet the man of my dreams. Fall in love, have a family. Casey Lynn could help. She knew a lot of people and maybe she could introduce me to someone and we could double-date.

With about five months before school, I took a job at Highland Hospital, a psychiatric hospital in Asheville. The job provided me with day-shift work, the only kind of work I was willing to accept by then. Highland was ahead of its time. The hospital used a holistic approach, treating mind and body, and it looked more like a small college campus with charming buildings. There were tennis courts and nature trails. Good food and proper nutrition were high priorities. Highland today is perhaps best known for being the place where F. Scott Fitzgerald's wife Zelda died. She'd been in and out of the facility for about five years when, one night in 1948, a fire broke out in the kitchen. It spread through the dumbwaiter shaft. Zelda was in a room on the top floor, locked and with bars on the windows. She died along with eight others in the hospital.

Although Highland Hospital provided me with day-shift work, I didn't care for the job at all. It was much more supervision than nurturing care, and I felt more like a guard than a nurse. It didn't help that I was assigned to the adolescent floor. I wasn't much older than the patients and I was insecure in my role, something, of course, the patients could sense and exploit. I was harassed constantly.

But it was nice living with Casey Lynn, someone I was looking to more and more as a role model. By then, she had broken up with her boyfriend. At the end of the workday, I would come home and Casey Lynn would make me a drink. During the worst of my ulcer, I completely avoided alcohol, but now it seemed okay to do so. On especially bad days, I might have a second drink, sometimes a third. I hadn't noticed that Casey Lynn would have a drink or two even before I'd gotten home. My previous experience with drinking had actually been short-lived. A few years before, prior to the ulcer, I had picked up a bottle of red wine on an especially tense day. I had a glass. Then another. I liked the way my stress seemed to dissipate and I had a third. Soon the bottle of wine was gone, and, not long after that, I was throwing it all up, praying to God to take away my nausea and then to take away the ensuing headache. With Casey Lynn, the drinking was more measured but still immoderate. And it quickly became a regular thing. Somewhere along the line, it helped erode my inhibitions. One night in a hotel room, on a vacation with Casey Lynn to Gatlinburg, Tennessee, Casey Lynn kissed me again. This time it didn't stop with just a kiss. Casey Lynn and I became lovers, me reluctantly so.

CHAPTER 11

MAINE

I don't know to this day why Casey Lynn and I became lovers, except that I did love her. She was smart and sophisticated and independent, and she introduced me to so many things—poetry, music, art, different religious perspectives. She said she loved me, and of course I was deeply touched by that, by the idea that somebody could find me lovable. Dr. Mac had suggested I could be loved, but, until Casey Lynn, it had been more or less theoretical.

In the evenings, she'd often invite me into her large master bedroom suite, which was down in the cellar of the house, but the house was built on a hill and half the cellar was above ground and there were windows on that side. There was a birdfeeder near the windows and we'd watch the cardinals that would gather there. The room was decorated with white, French provincial furniture and there were comfortable chairs and a table. A bottle of wine would always appear and we'd listen to music. Sometimes she'd show me a poem by Robert Frost or Emily Dickenson. Often the evenings would end with us together in her bed. Casey Lynn was my first lover.

Once or twice a month, we would take trips someplace. We visited Charleston and toured Fort Sumter, where the first shots of the Civil War were fired. We visited the old slave markets and I stood in silence, contemplating the immense tragedy that took place in those markets—families split apart and sold piecemeal. This, after the loss of home and the unspeakable ocean voyages. We toured antebellum plantations, where the slaves had suffered physical and often sexual abuse. We saw *Porgy and Bess* in Charleston, an unforgettable performance by an African-American ensemble. I thought of the beautiful spirituals, the songs I had sung at camp, songs that had been created by the slaves of the South.

We visited Cades Cove in the Smokey Mountains. At Cherokee National Park we watched an outdoor performance of *Unto These Hills*, performed by Native Americans, which memorialized the Cherokee "Trail of Tears" when President Andrew Jackson had the Cherokee Nation forcibly removed from their ancestral homelands in the Southeast to designated Indian territories in Oklahoma, another sad chapter in American history.

Once we drove to Mount Mitchell, about twenty miles outside of Asheville. Casey Lynn loved the mountains and was proud of our mountain heritage and wanted me to be as well. Scotch-Irish immigrants, our people had come to America largely as indentured servants, settling in the mountains where they made honest livings. Mountain people, though Southern, stayed out of the Civil War, for the most part. They were not slave owners, as there were no plantations in the mountains. The rich "flatlanders," as Casey Lynn put it, were the slave owners. There were no major battles in the mountains either, the terrain too formidable for either side to venture into. At Mount Mitchell, Casey Lynn made a point of making sure I knew that it was the highest mountain east of the Mississippi, higher even than Mount Washington in New Hampshire.

On the trip, she announced to me that she had made me executor of her estate, and would leave most of it to me. She was only in her early forties and healthy, and the announcement puzzled me. Casey Lynn loved me and the gesture was sincere. Still, there was a part of it that was manipulative, something I couldn't see at the time. There were other small manipulations. Casey Lynn continually tried to talk me out of going to St. Joseph's in the fall. It was a diploma mill, she insisted. I should apply to college in Asheville, she would say.

She often commented on Northerners, saying that Yankee folk, including me, talked too fast and too loud, a result of living in crowded Northern cities. With this, I couldn't argue. Living in Asheville, I did come to appreciate Southern graciousness. Store clerks always smiled and ended every transaction with, "Y'all come back now."

I went on a retreat while I was in North Carolina, organized by the Episcopal church we had been attending in Asheville. It was my first retreat and I was taken by the essential, and mandatory, silence. The only speaking was by the priest, who would deliver talks and a blessing that he gave to each attendee. I enjoyed the daily routine of the retreat as well as the beautiful, serene mountain setting. Casey Lynn didn't come along and it gave me the opportunity to reflect on my relationship with her, as well as my future in North Carolina.

By September, I knew that when I went to Maine, I would not be coming back to live. I continued to hate my job at Highland Hospital and my relationship with Casey Lynn was not what I wanted. It had never felt exactly right, even from the start. We were supposed to meet men and double-date. That was the original idea. I still wanted a family. And I wanted a man, not a woman. I wanted a husband. I wanted children. What I had with Casey Lynn, even though I loved her, was not what I had ever intended.

I realized, too, that much of the social life in Asheville revolved around family and church. I was a Yankee with a Yankee accent. I had relations there, but I remained something of an outsider. The Episcopal church in Asheville was small and made up of a few families and mostly older parishioners. My future was not in Asheville. Dr. Mac had taught me to be responsible for my own happiness and I knew my happiness was not in North Carolina. Casey Lynn was deeply disappointed when September came and I left for Maine. But Dr. Mac had also taught me that I was not responsible for the happiness of others and that included Casey Lynn. We would keep in touch through occasional letters and we would see each other at family gatherings in Asheville, but the relationship we'd had when I lived in her home was over.

Before arriving at St. Joseph's in September, I stopped in Connecticut for a week. I needed to say goodbye to Brig and I needed to talk to Dr. Mac once more. Brig told me I was welcome in her house any time and to come see her on college break, which I would do. In Dr. Mac's office, I told him of my relationship with Casey Lynn. "Well, Sarah," he said, "you're young. Sexual experimentation isn't uncommon. It's okay to be open to new things. Be careful, though, not to categorize yourself by an experience. Remember to be aware of yourself and aware of what brings you joy and happiness." On my way out of his office, he told me his door would always be open to me.

I left for St. Joseph's and loved it immediately. Standish, Maine, where the college is located, is about a half-hour drive west of Portland and located on Sebago Lake. Across the lake to the west can be seen the Presidential Range of mountains in New Hampshire, including Mount Washington, beautiful if not quite as tall as Mount Mitchell. The sunsets over the lake behind the mountains were spectacular from St. Joseph's.

At the college, there were a couple of dorms set aside exclusively for the RN students who were going for their bachelor's degrees. We were all in our mid-twenties to mid-thirties, older than most of the undergraduates. Thanks to my savings, I was able to afford a private room, which I felt was necessary given that I was still waking up with the occasional nightmare. There were seven of us on my floor. Besides me, there was Beverly and Colleen from Boston, Darlene from north of Boston, Laura and Carol from Western Pennsylvania, and Gloria from New Jersey. We enjoyed each other's company and enjoyed sharing our respective nursing experiences.

We were all majoring in health administration and took many of the same required classes, often studying together. We were allowed a couple of elective courses, too, and I took US history and Shakespeare, which I loved. After working forty-hour weeks, holidays, and weekends, I found the college experience delightful. I made good grades. I made friends. I had more space in my room since I didn't have a roommate and often we'd hang out in my room and play Scrabble and order pizza. And I loved the beautiful grounds of the campus. Adding to the experience, I often skied during the winter at a resort near the New Hampshire border.

In Portland, I found an Episcopal cathedral with an outstanding choir, which I auditioned for, making the cut and becoming one of the choir's forty members. We rehearsed Thursday evenings and sang at the eleven o'clock Sunday morning services. I developed a crush on Mike, the young, handsome choir director. He had black hair and a neatly trimmed mustache and beard. With the support of my friends, I worked up the courage to ask him out for coffee one night after practice. He said he was sorry; there was someone else in his life, but I was proud of myself for having asked him out. It was the seventies, after all, and, prior to these times, women rarely asked men out.

The year went by fast. In no time at all, it was spring and I had to decide what I was going to do next and where I was going to go. I thought about staying, perhaps finding work in New Hampshire, where I could continue to appreciate the scenery and continue to ski in the winters. My three RN friends from the Boston area encouraged me to move to Boston with them. This sounded exciting. A big city with world-renowned hospitals. The Red Sox. The Celtics. And, more than anything, friends whom I knew. I listed the pros and cons of each move. I had two wonderful options: two places I felt could make me happy. I had never had such a choice before. But, after all of the loneliness I had experienced, the idea of having friends was one I dared not take for granted. I decided to move to Boston, excited to find the happiness there that had eluded me in Asheville.

CHAPTER 12

BOSTON

In Boston, Colleen was kind enough to let me stay at her three-story walkup until I could find a place of my own. What I found was a six-hundred square foot, one-bedroom apartment with off-street parking. Colleen had counseled me about Boston's street-parking—having to move your car for the street cleaners and having your car buried by the snowplows in winter or else towed. Off-street parking was valuable.

While with a temporary nursing agency, I got a position working as a private duty RN, tending to patients in their homes. Most of the patients were elderly, but one was a breast cancer patient in her fifties. I took care of her during the last week of her life. One day the pastor from the woman's church came by and spoke to the woman, even though by then she was unconscious. He spoke to her husband and children, too. Before he left, he invited them to hold her hands and join in a circle around her bed. The family, in turn, invited me to join them and then the pastor led us in the Lord's Prayer. When we finished, the woman was no longer breathing.

The woman's passing was a peaceful, quiet transition. I found it powerful and moving. These were the days before hospice care was common. Elisabeth Kübler Ross's influential book, *On Death and Dying*, had come out a few years before, but the hospice movement was only in its infancy. In the hospital setting, I had witnessed how dying patients were routinely avoided by both the nurses and the doctors. When treatments and medications were no longer effective and the patients were too sick to be sent home, an awkwardness came over the hospital staff. Without a private duty nurse, the patients were given minimal care.

The experience in the woman's home confirmed for me a sense that I had had that these moments of transition were holy. If it can be called beautiful, her death was that. For my part, I would always give the best care to the dying that I knew how to give.

On Death and Dying was one of many books I had read or was reading about that time. My discovery of reading, a direct function of my learning that my IQ was above average—that I was not, as I had assumed, stupid—led me to learn and grow on my own, outside of classrooms and work. I could read about, and thereby learn about, anything that happened to pique my curiosity, opening whole new worlds for me. *Everything You Always Wanted to Know about Sex: But Were Afraid to Ask* was the huge bestseller of the times, and I made sure to read a copy. Wayne Dyer's *Your Erroneous Zones* was out, too: "Step-by-Step advice for escaping the trap of negative thinking." Somewhere in my readings, I came across *Desiderata*, the poem by Max Ehrmann. "You are a child of the universe no less than the trees and the stars; you have a right to be here." This was a stunning and beautiful thought. *I had a right to be here.*

As in Asheville, my main priority in Boston was to meet a wonderful man, fall in love, get married, and start a family. Working as a nurse made this difficult. One never knew what one's schedule was going to be. Monthly rotating schedules sometimes meant day shifts, sometimes evening shifts, sometimes the dreaded night shifts, of which I wanted no part. It was weekends and holidays, too. It was almost impossible to get into a routine or to commit to any kind of social activity. Eventually, I found a position at a student health center at a large Boston university, working 8:30 a.m. to 4:30 p.m. every day, with weekends and holidays off. The favorable hours came with a price: the pay was about half of what it would have been for a comparable hospital nursing position. My salary was ten-thousand dollars a year, low even for those times. Budgeting in a city like Boston was a challenge, but I figured if the college students could make it work, so could I.

There was a women's health clinic at the center and the patients were mostly students and many of the appointments were for birth control (the pill had only recently made its appearance), sexually transmitted diseases, and unplanned pregnancies. Valerie was a public health nurse for the clinic and we became good friends. She and her husband Marty were from Chicago. Valerie had worked as a public health nurse in the South Side of Chicago, tending to people in their apartments in the projects. She enjoyed the independence and the nursing challenge of caring and advocating for her patients. Now she was finishing her master's degree. Marty had a day job as an engineer, but he was an artist and furniture designer at heart. He'd constructed the furniture in their living room, a couch and chairs whimsically fashioned out of PVC pipe and cushions.

Val was always smiling and laughing. She told funny, sometimes harrowing, stories of working as a nurse in the projects of Chicago's South Side. She and her husband didn't make much money, but they were resourceful and made frugality into a game to be enjoyed. They had no car and Marty rode a bike to work. "We need to think creatively," Val would always say, and she carried this attitude into all facets of her life. It was advice she would give me whenever she saw me losing patience with something. Val enjoyed life and I thought of her attitude and how it contrasted with the unhappy attitude of my family when I was growing up, a family with plenty of money and no need to think creatively. Once, Val asked me who my support system was. I didn't know people had support systems. Val grew up in Chicago, in a big Polish family with lots of uncles and aunts and cousins. I didn't have that. Finally, after thinking long and hard, I told her my support systems were my friends and my faith journey in the Church.

Val was a skilled practitioner and popular with the students. She was also a proficient cook and she considered someday starting a restaurant. When she learned I hadn't celebrated my birthday for three years, not since I'd last lived in Connecticut, where the only person who would take the trouble to arrange for a small party was Lillian, she made me an eighteen-layer torte, which had to have taken the better part of a day to create. She brought it into work and surprised me with it in the break room over lunch, with the whole staff singing happy birthday to me.

I found an Episcopal church in Boston, the historic Church of the Advent, a wonderful place of worship that emulated the Catholic Mass within the Anglican tradition. The church had a large steeple, with eight change-ring bells. The sanctuary was a traditional Victorian Gothic that had phenomenal acoustics and a famous Aeolian-Skinner pipe organ. When the organ played, you felt as if you were in the anterior room of Heaven itself. The choir consisted of thirty professional voices and the worship experience would have been deeply moving by way of the music alone. There was a healing service, too, every Wednesday evening in the Our Lady Chapel, which was typically attended by just twelve or fifteen parishioners. Through the Church of the Advent, I felt a deeper spirituality than I had ever felt before.

After Sunday service, I would walk across the Boston Common and have breakfast at a muffin shop on Tremont Street and read the

Boston Globe. I loved living in Boston. I loved the ethnic diversity, the Italian North End, the Irish Southeast, known as Southie, the eclectic restaurants—Thai, Mexican, Vietnamese, Haitian, all foods I had never experienced growing up in my white bread neighborhood. I learned to ride the subway, a new experience for me. I loved the history of the city, the museums, the harbor. I loved the music. Colleen and I would attend the rehearsals of the Boston Symphony, which were cheap to get into. We also signed up for adult education programs, which allowed us to procure student ID cards and get the typical student discounts on admission to various places.

At one point, a friend of mine from the clinic was struggling financially and needed a place to live. I invited her to stay in my tiny apartment and we brought in an extra single bed. What I didn't know was that Wanda was an alcoholic. I tried to set boundaries; I didn't want to be an enabler. It was difficult and I found myself asking the priest at the church for guidance. Things only became more complicated, and a whole lot more crowded, when my sister moved in. Brenda had just received her MBA and had come to Boston looking for a job. It's strange, looking back. Through everything, I was still holding myself responsible for her, willingly taking on the role of big sister, looking out for her. Several years earlier in Waterbury, I'd done something similar after she'd had her tonsils removed, a painful operation for an adult. I had become a special nurse to her, a designation more or less equivalent to a private duty nurse. And now here I was in Boston, taking her into my miniature flat even though I already had a roommate, and a high-maintenance one at that. But it was more than just a feeling of responsibility. It was a deep-seated need for family. Eventually, Wanda moved out, feeling squeezed by Brenda and me, and aggravated by my boundaries. Brenda soon followed and I had the apartment to myself once again.

One day I heard from my father. I hadn't seen him since the time we went to see *Man of La Mancha* together. He'd sent me a few Christmas gifts in the years since, an expensive perfume set one year that I threw away, and boxes of cookies for a couple of years after that. I ate the cookies and then hated myself for eating them. My father had sold our house and moved into an even more expensive house in a gated community on a golf course in Farmington, Connecticut. This was the first I'd ever heard of gated communities. In the process, without telling us, he'd sold most of our things. My bike, my dolls, pictures from camp, pictures of my aunt and grandmother, everything in my old bedroom was gone. Thankfully, I had my guitar and jewelry box, with my Miraculous Medal, along with a nativity set that I had, over my childhood years, bought piece by piece at Woolworths at nineteen cents apiece. Nineteen cents for the baby Jesus, nineteen cents for the Blessed Mary, for Saint Joseph, for the shepherds, for the wise men. Improbably, I had taken the set with me to nursing school; otherwise, my father would have tossed it as well.

I visited my father in Farmington. His new top-of-the-line Cadillac was parked in the driveway. There was a card table in the kitchen, with two folding chairs, and, in the master bedroom, there was a bed, a chair, and a TV, and that was the extent of the furniture in the house. "I'm diversifying into real estate," he explained, "and the house is an investment. I don't want a lot of stuff in here, making the place looked used." He introduced me to his new girlfriend. It was she, in fact, who'd insisted that my father get in touch with me so that we could meet. He would not otherwise have bothered. Another girlfriend would follow not long after that. My father would tell me once that he never broke up with women. If he wanted to stop seeing them, he'd just do things that he knew would make them angry and eventually they would leave.

Meanwhile, Val graduated and she and Marty moved back to Chicago. She had not only introduced me to the concept of a support system, she had become a large part of my own. Not long afterwards, I began getting sharp pains in my back, shooting down my left leg. It would only be years later, looking back on it, that I would tie the back problems to Val's moving away. My sadness over her departure manifested itself as physical pain. Adding to it, I was still distraught over my father's tossing away of my childhood mementos. My body caved. I was put on bed rest, the standard course of action for back pain then, and the director of the university was good enough to allow me to be a patient in the infirmary. I was there for five days and then sent home with a prescription for Percocet. After a couple of months, there was only minor improvement. I got through the days working at the health center and then came home, where I would lie in bed with a hot pack. I slept poorly. I lost weight.

I had a myelogram done and was told I had a disk rupture, but that it was too small to operate on, and I began to think I had a chronic problem for which there would be no cure. Then I remembered Brig and her own brand of self-administered physical therapy. I did research and found books on back pain and back exercises. I realized that, since I'd moved to the city, I had stopped taking the long walks I used to enjoy. I hadn't been skiing regularly either. I'd been less physically active all the way around. I started walking more and developed my own exercise regimen and over the months, my back pain lessened considerably.

Despite the improvement, I found my mood getting worse. I was often irritable and depressed. I drove down to Meriden and saw Dr. Mac. We talked. Then he put me on a tricyclic antidepressant, which helped. Not long after that, I found a small women's Episcopal retreat about twenty-five miles north of Boston. Ever since the retreat in North Carolina, I had wanted to go on another. It was in another quiet, wooded area and I found it just as valuable, just as cleansing.

The retreat improved my overall mood, but I was becoming frustrated at work by then. I knew that our health services center could do so much more with student health education than what it was doing. It seemed to me as if we were missing an opportunity to better inform the students with pamphlets about birth control and other health issues. My supervisor disagreed and rather than remain frustrated, I began searching for another job, finding one eventually at Boston City Hospital.

Boston City Hospital was founded in 1864 in the South End "for the poor and indigent," according to its charter. It was still largely for people with few resources. If you had insufficient insurance to be admitted to one of the other hospitals, you'd be taken to Boston City Hospital. I worked as a continuing care nurse, evaluating patients who needed ongoing care after hospital discharge and determining whether they should be sent to a rehabilitation facility or nursing home. Sometimes they'd be sent to a chronic disease hospital on Long Island in Boston. I'd evaluate them in an eighteen-bed ward, all eighteen beds in one enormous room. Many of the patients were homeless alcoholics. I had never known people like that before; I had never known people who slept outdoors.

I often had to follow up on the patients and I'd find myself visiting them in the nursing homes we would send them to in Dorchester or Roxbury, tough parts of town. This was right at the time that school busing had become an explosive issue in Boston. A court order had mandated that the schools be desegregated. White students were to be bussed to black sections of town and black students were to be bussed to white sections. The court order did not go over well. Racial violence exploded in the city's poorer sections. These were the sections I had to drive through. I would swelter in the summer heat, keeping the windows up in my un-air-conditioned car as I made my way through them. The hospital itself was in a tough neighborhood. A car was set on fire one night in our parking area.

I needed a change. In the meantime, I was still without the family I wanted. Friends were getting married and having children while the years were passing me by. Somewhere along the line, still not where I wanted to be in life, still often struggling with depression, still tethered to my childhood in ways I could not then have understood, I turned thirty.

CHAPTER 13

TOM

Nothing changed. I continued working at Boston City Hospital as the months came and went and another year rolled by. I had vacation time scheduled for the end of the summer, right around my thirty-first birthday and the Labor Day weekend. Single friends of mine from the hospital had already taken their vacations. I wanted to go somewhere, but it would have to be by myself. I didn't want to go to a couple's destination or on a bus tour with seniors. And I didn't want to go to Asheville, my traditional go-to place. I was trying to grow, trying to be mature. I wanted to step out on my own. And I was still intent on heeding Dr. Mac's admonition, trying to be responsible for my own happiness. But where could a single woman go?

In the newspaper, I spotted an ad for a windjammer cruise—tall sailing ships that sailed out of Camden and Rockland, Maine. The ships cruised around Penobscot Bay, anchoring in the harbors of charming villages along the Maine coast or sailing to islands that dotted the bay. I'd never lost my love of sailing since the summer sailing camps, and, in fact, belonged to a sailing club in Boston. I'd passed a sailing test and was deemed qualified to take out the club's eighteen-foot sloops on the Charles River. I loved sailing and I loved Maine. The windjammer cruise seemed perfect.

There were twenty-eight passengers aboard our boat, a 120-foot schooner named the *Mary Day*. The passengers were a mix of singles and couples, ages ranging from twenties to late seventies, roughly half men and half women. My cabin mate was another single woman in her twenties. The cabin was cozy and I slept better than I ever had, lulled to sleep every night by the gentle rocking of the boat. Every morning, after a full breakfast prepared by the captain's wife on a wood stove, the passengers were invited to help haul up the anchor and hoist the sails, and then it would be off to wherever the wind and tide would take us. I loved the movement of the ship and the quiet power and beauty of the sails. I'd find an undisturbed corner of the ship somewhere and read and enjoy the serenity, looking out over the beauty of the sea, spying the tall pine trees on the island shores. A couple of times during the trip, we'd pass by a lighthouse standing guard for the mariners navigating the waters.

We'd have lunch on board and there was always a mid-afternoon happy hour. Typically, we'd put into port somewhere, and, after dinner, we'd go ashore and walk around whatever charming island we happened to sail to. On some of the islands, we'd double the population by our presence. Lobster fishermen made their homes on the islands and the kids would have to take a ferry to the mainland for school. Mail and groceries came by boat and were usually made available to the residents in somebody's charming home—a general store/post office downstairs, the living area upstairs. We'd grab a newspaper to keep abreast of world events, but I couldn't muster any interest in what was going on elsewhere. Once, we saw they were having a heat wave in New York City, temperatures above one-hundred degrees. We were in long pants and sweatshirts, the temperatures in the evenings around Penobscot Bay often hovering in the low sixties. The sunsets were spectacular, and, at night, looking up between the masts, into the dark, clear sky above, the tiny, diamond stars of the Milky Way produced a narrow, glowing beach in the sky. One cannot see a sky so rich with stars in the city.

Anchored in port one day, the captain happened to mention that, if anybody wanted to jump overboard into the water, they were welcome to. It happened to be my birthday, and, in celebration of the day, I jumped from the high gunwale of the ship, ten feet into the water below. The frigid sea took my breath away the moment I plunged into it. I had no idea it would be as cold as it was. I managed to swim to the boat's rope ladder and make it back up to the deck, trembling and turning blue. Other passengers tossed dry towels in my direction. A retired lawyer in his seventies brought me a glass of what turned out to be whiskey. "Drink this," he said. "It'll warm you up." I gulped it like it was a soda. I eventually warmed up, and then we all laughed about it. Not for one moment did I feel self-conscious. Among these people, on this wonderful vacation in this magical spot, I felt comfortable and safe. It was like sailing camp again and I felt as if I could be myself.

When the trip finally ended, I found myself in need of a ride back to Boston. I'd left my car with my sister. Two guys from the cruise, Tom and his housemate Joe, who lived in a suburban town about twelve miles north of Boston, offered to take me. Tom's car didn't have air conditioning. It was hot and the Labor Day traffic was terrible. We rolled the windows down hoping for relief. There was a cooler of beer in the car and Tom and Joe were both drinking as we drove along. I sat in the backseat, praying to be delivered home safely, regretting my decision to place my trust in these two men, angry at myself once again for my poor judgment.

Tom had to drop Joe off at their house first. Joe was divorced and his ex-wife was coming by with the kids. The house was owned by Tom and he invited me in when we got there. The first thing I noticed was the curtains in the front windows—pop-tops from beer cans, all strung together. Inside there was a nine-foot bar in the living room and more pop-top curtains in the dining room. I didn't stay long before asking Tom if we could please just continue on to my apartment. I made him drop me off at a subway stop, not wanting him to know where I lived.

The next week, Tom called and asked me out on a date. I told him I was busy. A few days later, he tried again. This time I told him I had plans to go on a religious retreat. I figured he'd find that a turnoff, but instead he insisted that we at least meet up somewhere so he could show me the pictures he'd taken on the cruise. I agreed to meet him in Boston's Kenmore Square the next evening. Tom was charming, with his easy sense of humor and dry wit, and I found myself enjoying my time with him. He made me laugh and we had a pleasant evening together. Afterwards, he asked me out again. "I like you, Tom," I said, "but we have a problem. I don't care for the drinking. I work at Boston City, you know. I see the people who come in there, many of them alcoholics. I send them to rehabilitation facilities. I pass by the drunks in Boston Common. The drinking is just something I'm not comfortable with. The cooler in your car, the bar in your house, the pop-top curtains…"

"That's not a problem," Tom smiled. "I could stop drinking if it's really an issue for you." I said that it was, but there was another issue that I didn't tell Tom about. Right before the cruise, I had broken up with a guy. He had been the first man with whom I'd had the normal sexual experiences of adult men and women. We'd broken up mostly because he didn't want children. I wasn't sure if I wanted to get into another relationship, but Tom seemed so sincere. I relented, and, as far as the drinking went, Tom was as good as his word. We started to date, and, for at least a month, he didn't have a drink. We'd go out and we'd both order an iced tea or soda. Tom had no plans to quit entirely, and I would never have demanded he do so, but the month without alcohol relieved me of some of my concerns. In the meantime, he was nice and fun to be with. I met his friends and I liked them. When Joe would have his kids over, he'd sometimes have to leave them with Tom when he went to work and I enjoyed watching how Tom interacted with them. He kept a toy box in the house for them. Before long, I met Tom's mother and sister and I liked how he treated them. I met a lot more of his family soon after at their annual family party, and they all seemed welcoming and genuine. Tom had a decent job and was a hard worker. He was clearly a good guy. I began falling for him, and he for me.

We had met in August, and, by Christmas, we were engaged to be married. It had happened quickly, but I was thirty-one and Tom was thirty-five and both of us had dated enough to know what we wanted. Tom, I'd learned, was coming off a broken engagement. We were both ready for commitment. I met his large Italian family at their annual Christmas party and spent the holiday with them, feeling more at home with them then I'd ever felt with my own family. We set a date for the wedding in May—Mother's Day, 1979, the only date we could get the reception venue for. And we set a place—the historic Church of the Advent.

My parents had each remarried by then. I had been invited to my mother's wedding, but not to my father's. My mother met Tom at a wedding shower that his mom was kind enough to throw for me. I introduced Tom to my father at my father's palatial house in Connecticut. The meeting was Cynthia's idea, my father's new wife. I liked Cynthia and I called her to tell her of my engagement and she insisted we come see them. Cynthia was in her late thirties, not that much older than me. She'd worked as a waitress and had two children, ages seven and nine, from a former marriage. She was an attractive blonde and outgoing and made the perfect housekeeper and cook and social secretary for my father—just what he was looking for. For his part, he was willing to take on the children. I thought about the dangers, but the children were both boys and I felt they'd be safe from him. Cynthia would later tell me that, before they married, my father had made her sign a prenuptial agreement, a relatively new legal instrument in those days. Just like my father to be in front of the curve when it came to taking care of his financial resources.

We had dinner at their new house on a rainy night. They had bought the house together and Cynthia had taken charge of the interior decorating and the place was beautiful. At Tom's and my place setting at the dinner table was a card and a check for one thousand dollars for our wedding. I knew the gift had to be Cynthia's idea, who seemed genuinely excited for us. My father said nothing, but I thanked them both.

After dinner, my father asked me to follow him out to his detached four-car garage to show me his antique Cadillac. When we were alone in the garage, he reached over and pulled me toward him and tried to kiss me on the mouth. I recoiled and ran back into the house, through the pouring rain. Soaking wet, I found myself standing on the mat just inside the door, unable to move, looking at the polished wood floor before me and repeating mindlessly, "I'm not dripping on the beautiful floors." It was all I could seem to wrap my mind around in that moment—not to drip on the floors. Finally, I collected myself and called Tom aside and told him we needed to leave.

Tom didn't ask why I wanted to leave so quickly, and I didn't explain, aside from mumbling something about our long two-hour, rainy drive back to Boston. I hadn't told Tom anything about my childhood, about my father and the abuse. In my mind, my father was no longer an issue. I had been dealing with my own problems and my own depression, seeing Dr. Mac and trying to fix my social difficulties. And now I had found the man of my dreams. I had turned a new leaf. The past was past.

But of course the effects of those years lingered in my subconscious. I'd never gotten past my anxieties. I had trouble having sex with Tom without taking a valium first or having a drink. Only then would I become comfortable enough to allow Tom to touch me sexually. But I never told him about my past history. It had been buried, as far as I was concerned. That night in my father's garage had horrifyingly brought it back, but I kept the feelings to myself. I wasn't trying to conceal anything from Tom. I really thought I had moved past it.

After that night, I didn't want to see my father again, but I held open my wedding invitation to him, thinking that his absence would create too many questions. I was still so concerned about what others thought. I still wanted to be accepted, to belong. I wanted to do the right thing, whatever that was. Inviting one's father to one's wedding seemed like the right thing. It was certainly traditional, and the wedding of my dreams, which is what I wanted, naturally had to follow tradition: my father would walk me down the aisle. For my mother's part, she planned to attend the wedding but told me a couple of weeks leading up to it that she would not be staying for the reception, not as long as my father was there. "Please come to the reception," I said. "I have a table for you and everything." It was a table for her and her husband Russell and three other couples, all people she knew and could be comfortable with, a table that was on the opposite side of the venue from my father's table. I held out hope she'd change her mind.

I mostly paid for the wedding out of my own savings and, on a limited budget, bought my wedding gown at a deep discount during Boston's annual "Running of the Brides." Every year, Filene's Basement, a downtown department store, would greatly mark down wedding dresses for a single day and hundreds of prospective brides would charge the store when it opened at 8:00 a.m. I went with my maid of honor and it was crazy and fun, and I ended up with a beautiful Bianchi gown I could not have afforded otherwise.

The wedding was wonderful. I dressed in my humble apartment with my mother, sister, and two bridesmaids. The photographer came to the apartment and took pictures. Tom's housemate and best man Joe drove me to the church. Tom's family were strict Catholics, but the Episcopal Church of the Advent had enough Catholic-like elements to fool at least Tom's elderly aunt, who commented that it was "the most beautiful Catholic church" she'd ever been in. A friend of mine played the organ. My father was there. My mother was stunning as usual in her standard ensemble of beautiful jewelry and fashionable dress and shoes. After the ceremony, she said goodbye to me on the church steps, with me imploring her one more time to change her mind and come to the reception. She shook her head and turned and walked away. Tom and I were driven to the reception in Tom's 1962 aqua-blue convertible Chevy Impala. I saw the empty table I had reserved for my mother and excused myself to go to the bathroom, where I cried, just as my mother had cried at her own wedding at the hands of her mother. Then I washed my face and determined that my mother was not going to ruin my wedding day, even as the guests noticed the empty table, many of them asking, "Sarah, where's your mother? Is she okay?"

Six months later, my sister was married in King of Prussia, Pennsylvania. I was her maid of honor, as she had been mine. My mother, with Russell, attended both the wedding ceremony and the reception, even though my father was at both with Cynthia. They even spoke to each other. My mother paid for a suite for the wedding party at the Sheraton and for a Rolls Royce limo for the bride and groom. Brenda and I both received tea sets from her as wedding gifts that year. Mine was plain pewter. Brenda's was silver, elaborate and gorgeous.

CHAPTER 14

FAMILY

Tom and I honeymooned in Bermuda and then I packed up my apartment to move into Tom's house. I cried when I closed the apartment door behind me for the last time. These were complicated tears. I had been challenged so much in the years since initially dropping out of nursing school at nineteen. And I had grown. I had changed. I was now closing the door on a sad and difficult era of my life and opening the door to the dream I had always wished for. I was grateful, yet anxious, hopeful that our love would grow, and Tom and I would enjoy our new life together.

Tom had bought his house from his Italian uncle Ren, short for Renaldo. Ren was his mother's brother, one of ten siblings—six boys and four girls—of which his mother was the eldest. Their parents—Tom's grandparents—had come from Italy in 1906, arriving at Ellis Island and eventually connecting with family in Boston, living in the north end.

Lots of aunts and uncles meant lots of cousins. Tom had twenty-two first cousins (five more on his father's side). I had met many of them at that Christmas party where I'd first been introduced to Tom's family. The annual event had been started in 1960 by Tom's Uncle Norman and Norman's beautiful Norwegian wife Margit. Margit had come to the United States after her father had been killed in World War II following the Russian invasion of Norway. He'd been working to smuggle Jews out of the country. One of the last things he'd told his daughter was that she had to get out of the country. "There's no future for you here," he'd said.

Margit had been a nurse. While learning English, she became a nanny for famed Boston Pops conductor Arthur Fiedler and she eventually acquired her nursing license in the United States. Ultimately, she saved enough money to open a residential home for private-pay elderly women with comfortable rooms where the residents could have their own furniture, putting her on the forefront of the assisted living industry. From there, Margit went into real estate and she did extraordinarily well, a poster child for the American dream. The annual family parties at her and Norman's luxurious house were elaborate, catered affairs, with tables of food, including fifteen or twenty different kinds of desserts. With years separating Tom's aunts and uncles, family members of all ages attended the party. That's where new members were always introduced, whether fiancés or babies. Coming from my small family, it was quite a shock, one I found delightful. Everyone was warm and welcoming and I was thrilled to be a part of Tom's family.

Carmella, Tom's mother, was seventy-one when we got married, while my own mother was only in her fifties. Carmella was smart, despite having dropped out of school after eighth grade to help support her large family, taking a job as a bookkeeper. Eventually, she acquired her GED and then went on to earn a nursing home administrator's license. Somewhere in the 1960s, her and her brothers pooled their money together and bought a thirty-two-bed rest home. Carmella was incredibly hardworking. Had she grown up with today's opportunities for women, I imagine she probably would have been a CEO somewhere.

There were always funny stories told about the nursing home. Truly, it was a family affair. There was an upstairs apartment in the home that was made available to family members or friends who might need a place for a short stay. Sometimes, if the cook called in sick, Tom would be enlisted to take over the kitchen duties, having learned some cooking skills growing up. Tom's father sometimes did the bookkeeping.

Tom's father was of Irish descent. He'd worked in the Fore River shipyards during World War II and had a variety of different blue-collar jobs while Tom was growing up. Eventually he was diagnosed with Buerger's disease, a chronic disease of poor circulation and inflammation of the arms and legs, exacerbated by his two-pack-a-day cigarette habit. He died five years before Tom and I were married.

Tom's oldest sister, Lisa, was born with Turner syndrome, a rare chromosome disorder that can lead to a variety of developmental problems. The disease went undiagnosed for the longest time. At two weeks, her lack of development was such that the doctor admitted to being surprised she was still alive. She wouldn't live to be three months, was the prognosis. At three months, the prognosis was six months. At six months, it was a year.

The family was religious and prayed for her constantly. Lisa kept surprising everybody, but she remained sickly and small. The family lived at that time in a small rural town south of Boston. They had no car and Tom's mother would have to take the "T" subway system, getting a ride first from a neighbor or taking a bus to the nearest station, then having to make two changes on the T to finally get to Massachusetts General. There, the doctors were continually amazed by Lisa's survival. At age seven she weighed just twenty-seven pounds, but she kept on surviving. It wouldn't be until her thirties that doctors finally stopped making projections about her longevity.

Lisa would, in fact, live to be sixty, but her life was a hard one. She was tiny—four-feet ten inches—and her bones were weak and easily broken. She had three hip replacements and multiple bone fractures. It seemed she was always in a leg or arm cast. She was also infertile, having never made it developmentally to puberty. She never married, but was fortunate to attend LPN school to become a nurse. I met her and was amazed by her grace and by her acceptance of her condition. "Don't you ever get depressed?" I asked her one time.

"Why would I?" she replied. "Look at how much God and my family love me."

Tom's house was a small, charming, two-bedroom Craftsman-style bungalow with high, molded ceilings and built-in corner china cabinets. There were porches on both the front and back of the house. I was thrilled to be out of the apartments. I loved the quiet and the privacy of our home, the luxury of not being able to hear the neighbor's stereo. Interest rates were up around eighteen percent at the time and most of my friends couldn't afford houses. But the house needed some tender loving care. As a new bride, one of my first goals was to improve the housekeeping and the interior decor. I started with the pop-top curtains. Out they went. Tom insisted the nine-foot bar remain and I gave in on that. We both agreed to have the kitchen redone. In no time, the house felt like home, with me and Tom and Tom's cat Hermie. Hermie had actually been another selling point for me on the marriage. Anybody who was an animal lover was okay in my book.

I changed jobs around that time, taking a position at a teaching hospital in Boston. There was a part-time opening in the maternity ward and since I'd begun thinking of having children, I figured it was a good way to learn more about babies, which, truthfully, I found a little intimidating. I still hadn't forgotten my experience with Amanda's three month old, her crying and my screaming back at her. I wanted to be a good mom. The job was for thirty-two hours a week, but Tom made decent money as a civil engineer for a firm in Boston and we lived comfortably.

For our first anniversary, we went back on a windjammer cruise. Some of the people from the previous cruise were aboard and we had a wonderful time, even though it rained for much of the week, making things a bit damp on the boat. We also went on a vacation to the UK that year, touring London and Ireland.

Tom and I both wanted a family, but, after a year of trying, I was still not pregnant. We had a fertility work-up done and no reason could be found other than apparently we weren't having sex often enough. That had to do with me. It was still not easy for me to have sex, still not easy for me to relax and enjoy the experience.

There was some stress with the job, too, and I decided to cut back on my hours. I began thinking that if I didn't soon get pregnant, I'd have to leave maternity. It was depressing and frustrating seeing other pregnant women, especially fifteen- and sixteen-year-old drug addicts who'd gotten pregnant by accident while I could not get pregnant on purpose, despite keeping charts of my ovulation schedule and having sex at the right times even if doing so began to feel perfunctory. I became obsessed with my perception of the unfairness of it all. And in the meantime, I felt terrible for Tom, whom I knew wanted a family at least as much as I did. I couldn't help feeling as if our problems were my fault.

Fertility drugs were in their infancy in those days and in some cases there had been complications, including premature birth. I had taken care of enough premature babies to understand the struggle and the stress endured by both baby and parents. I determined not to put my baby, or Tom and me, through that. I decided against the drugs. Instead, on my birthday that year, I bought myself a new Bible and told myself I was going to accept God's will. If I was meant to become pregnant, then it would happen. But I knew the clock was ticking. By then, I was thirty-four.

CHAPTER 15

VISITATION

It was October of 1981 and my period was two weeks late. There was no drugstore pregnancy test in those days so I made an appointment with my OBGYN. He did a urine test and the results came back two days later: I was pregnant. The baby was due the following July, and Tom and I were ecstatic.

I kept the pregnancy a secret. There were a couple nurses I worked with who'd had miscarriages and I became anxious. I knew that, in the first twelve weeks, a miscarriage was not all that uncommon. At ten weeks, I heard the baby's heartbeat and it gave me a thrill, but, after twenty weeks, I still hadn't told anybody. Tom and I were the only ones who knew. I was starting to show, but my hospital scrubs covered it up. I had an ultrasound done, a new procedure back then, and the picture showed a healthy baby growing in my womb. I took the picture and placed it in the bible I had bought for myself just a few months before, giving thanks and offering prayers. The picture remains there to this day.

Finally, I broke the news when a couple of the nurses asked. The scrubs could only hide so much and these were maternity nurses, after all. Still, I found myself unduly anxious about the baby. Part of the problem came from my experience as a nurse, seeing sickness, miscarriages, deformities, even stillbirths. I tried to do everything right. I didn't drink or smoke. I ate healthy. Eventually, while interviewing pediatricians, I found a female doctor with whom I felt comfortable sharing my concerns. "Sarah," she said, "you have a ninety-seven-percent chance of everything going one-hundred-percent right." Hearing the odds in clinical, rational terms greatly helped. So did my daily prayers and Scripture readings.

As it happened, Brenda had become pregnant two months before me. We talked often throughout our pregnancies, sharing our experiences. We bonded in a way we never had before. Meanwhile, I tried talking with my mother. I'd ask her about her own childbirth experiences, but she was always vague. "They weren't too bad," she would say, and then change the subject.

To prepare for the delivery, Tom and I attended childbirth classes. It was a new thing for dads to be invited into the delivery room. We were both excited. The film *Chariots of Fire* was popular at the time and I loved the music and I visualized that labor would be like a long-distance run as depicted in the movie. Probably more like a full marathon, in fact. At the end would be a baby, the best prize of all. But toward the end of my pregnancy, I developed a cough severe enough to cause shortness of breath. After some tests, the doctors concluded I had asthma, most likely pregnancy-induced. I learned that somewhere around eight percent of pregnant women develop asthma.

I would have terrifying moments when I felt as if I was smothering. I couldn't lie down in my bed at night without the coughing starting up and I took to sleeping in a chair, sitting straight up. I would doze, but often I'd awake to more coughing and shortness of breath. The good news was that I was told the condition would abate after I gave birth. I later learned that women suffering from pregnancy-induced asthma, for whatever reason, frequently experience higher degrees of postpartum depression. I would also discover that, in Chinese medicine, respiratory issues are often believed to be associated with sorrow and grief. The asthma forced me to take a leave of absence earlier than I had planned, five weeks before I was due.

On my due date in July, Tom asked if he should stay home. Go to work, I told him, knowing that first-time moms seldom give birth on their due dates. Birth can be delayed a week or more. Sure enough, however, by noon that day, I was in labor. I called Tom, who came right home. Then, on a ninety-five-degree day in Boston, Tom drove me to the hospital in my small, blue, un-air-conditioned Chevette. My asthma more or less went into remission during labor, something my OBGYN had assured me would happen but something I'd been worried about just the same. How could I make it through labor if I couldn't breathe?

Everything went well, and, after nine hours of labor, our daughter was born. We named her Grace. I thought of the Visitation story in the Bible, where a pregnant Mary, mother of Jesus, visits a pregnant Elizabeth, mother of John the Baptist. Elizabeth was old and had come to believe she could not conceive a child. I was always moved by the grace that was bestowed on Elizabeth and I decided "Grace" would make a fitting name for our daughter.

The asthma hung on for a couple of months and then ultimately disappeared. Through my experience at the hospital, I felt ready to take care of a baby, but I was nevertheless humbled by the task. My pediatrician was supportive and I received the help I needed. But breastfeeding made me sore and was a challenge for me. I thought about quitting, but I knew that breast milk was healthier than formula. Still, I've since never judged any woman who decides against breastfeeding. I have come to learn that every woman does the best they can with the support they receive.

Then there was the lack of sleep, the missed meals, the interruption of routine. But through it all, I discovered a level of love for my beautiful daughter that I'd never experienced before. And I loved being a mom. I'd take Grace to the park, where I'd meet other moms and we'd share stories and tips.

I learned to soothe my daughter's cries, but when I couldn't console her with everything I'd learned as a post-partum nurse, and I was close to exhaustion, I'd put her in her crib, where I knew she would be safe and I would go outside of the house to get away from the crying, maybe even take a short walk around the yard. Never was it for any longer than fifteen minutes, but I was ever mindful of the time I had babysat my friend Amanda's three-month-old girl, screaming at her to shut up. I cringed, thinking of that incident, and swore never to repeat it, especially with my own daughter.

Tom was helpful in the evenings and nights. We would take turns walking Grace in a baby wrap that attached to our chests so she could hear our heartbeats. Tom would take her around the house, quietly talking to her and pointing out pictures and lamps and furniture, and bringing to her attention things outside the windows. He'd always make sure to show her our cats, too. We always had cats and they were always important to me. I found them comforting in the times when nobody else seemed to understand what was going on in my head. Many a night I was lulled to sleep by the purring of one of our cats curled up beside me in bed. Thankfully, Tom liked cats, too, and he enjoyed Grace's reaction to them. Finally, after a while in Tom's arms, being walked all around the house, Grace would fall asleep. Tom called the exercise "doing mileage."

Although my mother sent flowers, she didn't visit until Grace was over two months old. I longed for her to come earlier, to see her grandchild, to help and support me, to provide encouragement in those critical first few weeks in a way that only one's own mother could. Finally, she and my sister both came to see me. They stayed for a day. My mother told me she didn't like the name I had chosen for our baby. As a teacher, she'd had a troublesome student named Grace. They both came back again for the christening.

Three months after the birth, my maternity leave and vacation time was used up and I returned to work. A neighbor who was a mom with a five-year-old son was my childcare person and I switched to the 3:00 p.m. to 11:30 p.m. shift so that Grace would only be in childcare for three or four hours at a time. Tom could watch her once he got home from work. Plus, I only worked two days during the week. I worked weekends, but Tom watched Grace then.

My own experiences now of childbirth and new motherhood raised my level of confidence as a postpartum nurse. I felt especially blessed and honored now to be doing the work I was doing, helping new mothers with their newborns, showing them how to hold and feed them. I loved the teaching aspect of my work, explaining newborn behavior. Some of the mothers would be scared at first. Sometimes a baby would continue to cry and the mother would think her baby didn't like her, and I would assure her that was not true. The crying was normal. It was rewarding to comfort new moms and teach them how to comfort their babies.

In the meantime, Brenda gave birth to Michael, my nephew, two months before Grace came along. Just days after being discharged, Michael experienced neonatal jaundice and had to be re-hospitalized. My mother, who had offered to help with Michael initially, changed her mind when he was sent back to the hospital and didn't come. Brenda called me, terribly upset. I was seven-months pregnant at the time, but I went right down to see her, arranging for time off work. I assured her, based on what I knew as a maternity nurse, that, with the right care, Michael would be all right. I knew how traumatic it was for a new mother to see her baby re-hospitalized. I didn't spend too much time thinking about my mother's reaction, but I knew Brenda was stunned by it and I wondered if she could now see what I had seen my entire life—the lack of empathy and awareness and emotional availability.

But six months later, my mother decided to visit our grandmother at Aunt Iris's. Brenda and a now-healthy Michael were invited along. Grace and I were not. I found out about the trip afterwards and tried not to blame Brenda. How could she be blamed for being the favorite?

My father and his wife Cynthia came that fall to see Grace. At one point, my father held her and I saw his face flush and he had the look I had come to know as a child, the look of sexual desire. I felt as if my chest would explode and I snatched Grace from him, saying something about how he wasn't holding her quite right. I would never let him hold her again.

We were invited to my father's over Christmas that year, the invitation coming from Cynthia, of course. We went. I felt safe, given that Cynthia's two sons would be there as well as my father's brother Gene and his wife. During the gathering, Uncle Gene said to my father, "Chester, do you remember that time when your mother-in-law called the police on Sarah when she was a baby?" My father laughed, Gene laughed, everybody laughed. I sat bewildered, wondering why, in my infancy, the police had been called on me. And why was it funny? Then my father deflected, putting the blame on my grandmother. "What can you expect," he said, "from a woman who would always send loud toys to Sarah?" Then he admitted, laughingly, that more than once he'd had to toss out toys my grandmother had sent me, like a toy drum at Christmas one year. Everybody seemed to think that was funny, too.

But after the holidays, the new year brought hope in a way I had never felt before. Being a mother meant I mattered and I had never mattered before. Motherhood came with joys I'd never known. Even with all its anxieties, I decided I liked it.

My life: it actually mattered now.

CHAPTER 16

DEATH AND LIFE

In 1983, when Grace was eight months old, she developed a fever that rose to 105. I knew that, at such a high temperature, seizures could result, even brain damage. My real fear was meningitis. As a nurse, I knew too much. All the worst-case scenarios played out in my head. We rushed Grace to the hospital, where tests were performed, including a spinal tap.

In the special care nursery, I had helped doctors perform spinal taps on babies before and so I was not unfamiliar with the procedure. I stayed with Grace in the treatment room, holding her little body in the proper position and supporting her head while she cried nonstop. My pediatrician told me I could stay, but she made it clear that, if I wanted to leave, that would be okay, too. As familiar as I was with the process, it was still painful watching Grace in such discomfort, and I wished the doctor could perform the spinal tap on me instead. I initially decided to stay, but the thought of remaining in the room soon overwhelmed me and I turned to leave. As I did so, Grace cried harder. I held her until she calmed down and again I tried to leave. Again, she cried harder, and I realized that even though I'd have to be a witness to her pain, it would be more painful for her if I left. We went through the experience together and it awakened for me the idea that love is willing to share and endure the suffering of a beloved. This was a new idea to me.

After the procedure, back in the pediatric ward, I said my prayers and set my rosary next to Grace's crib, feeling otherwise helpless. I stayed with her, helping the nurses bathe her every two hours in luke-warm water, watching her skin turn a kind of gray-blue at times. I never left her room, dozing in the chair next to her bed every so often. Eventually, her fever came down, and she was ultimately diagnosed with a urinary tract infection. Antibiotics were administered via IV, and, three days later, Grace was able to come home, where she recovered without any complications.

In the spring, Tom and Grace and I traveled to Asheville to see my grandmother and Aunt Iris. Shortly after our marriage, Tom and I had traveled down and it had been Tom's first trip through the South. He'd commented on the preponderance of Baptist/Evangelical churches we had passed along the way. This was our first trip with Grace and we took dozens of pictures of her with my grandmother and my aunt. It was a wonderful time. But, at one point, my grandmother pulled me aside to tell me that my mother had asked for her engagement ring, the ring my grandmother had promised would one day be mine back when I was seven. She'd made the promise more than once to me, on nearly every visit since, in fact. The ring was only a quarter carat, but that didn't matter. It was the promise that had made me feel special and loved. It was a promise I had clung to ever since. Now it was to be my mother's ring. She'd manipulated my grandmother into breaking her promise. I nodded meekly as my grandmother spoke, too hurt and angry to say a word. Inside I was furious with my grandmother. Why couldn't she keep her promise to me? Later, I would come to see the situation for what it was—my mother, manipulating my grandmother who was vulnerable, because of her age and dependency. My mother, still finding ways to wound me.

That summer, when Grace was a year old, my sister and her husband came up with Michael and we all drove to the Cape, renting a house for a weekend and celebrating the birthdays of our children. It seemed important to be together with Brenda. It seemed important to try to be a family. On some level, I was still looking to be accepted, whether it was by Brenda, my mother, or even my father. They hadn't been proud of me in school with my mediocre grades. They hadn't been proud of me when I'd graduated from nursing school. They didn't seem impressed by my work or by my marriage. But now—certainly—they'd have to be impressed by Grace. They would have to love my daughter, even if they didn't love me. They'd have to see that I mattered now. The weekend was pleasant, but afterwards, as time went on, the distance between Brenda and me began to grow again. As the kids would get older, mostly out of feelings of obligation, we would vacation together at the Jersey shore in the summers. Eventually, the vacations to the shore would peter out as the kids would grow even older and busy schedules simply couldn't accommodate time together. The kids never grew close to each other to begin with, so there wasn't much that seemed lost.

That summer of 1983, when Grace was one year old, Tom and Grace and I traveled to Naugatuck to visit Brig, now in her eighties and still living in her charming home. We had tea and it was lovely to see her and a joy to know she was still doing well. She was delighted to meet Tom and to see Grace, who was walking by then.

That Christmas, against my better judgment, I went to my father's again, still feeling an obligation to the family. This time I prepared for the dinner by swilling a bottle of wine in the car as Tom drove us there. We arrived late and left early. Even in my inebriation, I kept a close eye on Grace, making sure my father got nowhere near her. That would be the last holiday I would spend with either of my parents.

My work at the hospital continued. I was close with my fellow nurses in the maternity ward, some of whom were older nurses who were grandmothers, and others who were younger, like me, and new mothers themselves. We all bonded and supported each other. Rachael, who was an art school student in addition to being a nurse, was an especially close friend. So was Pam, a student nurse who'd also come from a dysfunctional family and who was a single mom with a five-year-old son. One of the nurses on the floor, another close friend, was Robin. In late summer of 1983, Robin, younger than me at twenty-nine, had been diagnosed with breast cancer. She'd been separated from her husband and had a little two-year-old boy. Robin got no support from her own family and so when she could no longer work, we all did what we could to help her, the entire nursing and floor staff. We bought her groceries and clothes for her son, even cashing in our sick days and asking the hospital to send the checks to her. Eventually, Robin moved in with Pam.

We all started out thinking positively, but, as the weeks and months wore on, with Robin suffering through the chemo and the cancer ravaging her body, it became apparent she was not going to survive. In June of 1984, on her thirtieth birthday, she passed away. Just as heartbreaking as the death was what we all learned afterwards: nobody in Robin's family wanted to be responsible for her boy. They talked of foster care.

Pam, meanwhile, having roomed with Robin up until the end, took her death particularly hard. She had trouble functioning and trouble paying her bills. After checking with Tom, I asked Pam if she'd like to move into our place, just until she could get herself together again. For a month, she and her son squeezed themselves into our small home. It helped us both. In time, she moved in with another nurse—Ruth, a good friend of both of ours. Ruth had a big house and Pam and her son had their own bedroom and bath. Ruth lived farther out, however, and Pam had no transportation for work. Tom's mother was not well then and no longer drove and so we sold her car to Pam for one dollar.

What I didn't know at the time and would later learn was that Pam was struggling with other issues besides the death of Robin. As it happens, Pam, too, was an incest survivor. She'd been molested by an uncle. She was in therapy and had been hospitalized at one point after attempting suicide by slashing her wrists. Robin's death helped send her over the edge. All the while, my trajectory was paralleling hers. I was having trouble processing Robin's death, too. In fact, after Pam moved out, I found myself feeling anxious all the time. I started having intense nightmares. I constantly feared death and became obsessed with the idea that I would soon be killed, maybe in a car wreck or in some random criminal act. I was certain I had only weeks to live, maybe days.

It was as if I deserved to die because Robin had died. Robin was a wonderful person, young and vibrant. She was kind and funny, and it didn't make sense to me that she would die while I would live. Yes, I had come to believe that, as a mother, I mattered. But Robin was a mother, too. And I was one with secrets and shame and guilt. If God was just, then I would not be long for this world.

I finally had everything I'd ever wanted—a husband and a child. A family and a home. And now I was going to lose it all. I didn't deserve any of it, anyway. I began to get my affairs in order. I convinced Tom that we needed to write a will. I went to confession. For the first time, I confessed my father's abuse to a priest, the first time I had ever talked about it with anybody since I had described it so briefly to Dr. Mac years before when I was nineteen. The priest advised me to read the

Genesis story of Joseph, who was sold into slavery by his brothers, but who later saved them from famine and rose to become the most powerful man in Egypt, next to the pharaoh. I found the story very human and touching, and I understood the overarching idea of good coming from even the worst of circumstances, but the story did little to assuage the hidden shame I had never stopped feeling.

In fact, I found myself having anxiety attacks in church. As in childhood, I sat in the pew feeling sick and shameful. I felt the fear of God and the dread of hell. It was the fishhooks, tearing at my chest again. On several Sundays, I had to flee the sanctuary, unable to breathe.

I lived for months after Robin's funeral knowing I was the next to die. I began drinking more to help deal with the anxiety and, in truth, the survivor's guilt. There were days when I would call my daycare person and ask if I could drop off Grace for the day. Then I'd stay home and drink. Often I would sit with one of the cats in my lap, which was comforting. The dishes piled up. The laundry barely got done. Many nights I didn't make dinner. Soon I began to fear I would lose Tom. I was a mess; I was no longer the woman he married. If he left, he'd be sure to take Grace with him, and rightfully so. Then I would be alone in the world while Tom would find someone else to love, a new mother for Grace.

I became angry, too, and impatient, cursing in traffic and flying off the handle at the smallest of things. As the weeks rolled by and became months and I realized I was most likely not going to die, I knew I needed therapy again. Dr. Mac was too far away so I searched for a therapist nearby, one preferably with spiritual leanings. I found a Protestant psychologist in the next town. Ryan was younger than me and without extensive experience, but he had a doctorate and seemed competent. He asked me what I was angry about. The question surprised me because I hadn't seen myself as an angry person.

Nevertheless, I had a list of names, starting with my father and running all the way up to God.

I saw Ryan for about four months, but then one day he gave me three weeks' notice: he and his family were moving to New Hampshire. I took it personally and reacted with anger. I was hurt. I felt as if Ryan was abandoning me, and, once again, I felt betrayed. I was unkind and insulting to him. After his move, I made the two-hour drive to see him in New Hampshire, but I could never really get past the idea that he'd dared move away. The sessions were strained and one time we got into a shouting match. Ryan told me I was manipulative and narcissistic. Manipulative, because, in our early sessions, I would often bring him small token gifts. He was a new father and I'd often bring something small for his baby, from one parent to another. Looking back, I was probably trying to find some validation, some approval. Or, at the least, provide a small kindness to somebody. Maybe the motivation went back as far as childhood when I'd placed the dimes on my friends' driveways out of desperation and lack of self-worth. That he saw these acts of giving as manipulative was hurtful. And he thought I was narcissistic because I spoke of suicide. "Suicide is the most narcissistic act there is," he said. For me, my suicidal thoughts were never about me. I truly believed that Tom and Grace would be better off without me. Why couldn't Ryan understand that? As far as I was concerned, his accusations of manipulation and narcissism were just more negative labels spoken by a powerful man. One late, snowy December afternoon, I was driving home from Ryan's office in the dark, and the radio was playing "Jesu, Joy of Man's Desiring." I pulled over and openly wept. I prayed for guidance. I never saw Ryan again.

Fortunately, I still had my work to keep me going. Being a nurse gave me purpose; it gave me a function. I did it well. I felt as though it was the only worthwhile thing I could do. Once at the hospital, I snapped into work mode, dropping my thoughts about the outside world and the rest of my life. Once I changed into my blue scrubs, it was as if I became a different person. I was a *nurse*, and I was part of a larger group of nurses, all of us wearing the same blue scrubs. Work mended my threadbare, tattered self-esteem.

Nevertheless, I spiraled downhill after Ryan. My work notwithstanding, I was worthless and full of shame and ready to die. My nightmares got worse. One of them was a recurring dream of Grace dying in my arms, with me powerless to protect her. Her head was severed and rolling, blood everywhere. I would awaken screaming and then pace around the rest of the night, unable to go back to sleep. It occurred to me then that I was dragging Tom and Grace into my own hell. I needed to get away from these people whom I loved so dearly. They would have such a better life without me.

On a cold February day in 1985, fully prepared to kill myself, I desperately prayed once more, asking God what He wanted of me. "What do you want me to know today, God? I'm going to do it." It was in my daughter's room as she napped in her crib. I was considering hanging myself or perhaps dying of carbon monoxide poisoning. And that was when I had the vision where I was tied to a cross in a barren landscape, a silent killing field of souls, hung naked and dirty and filthy, close to death, the man in the clean, white tunic coming toward me—Jesus, come to take me, to pass his everlasting judgment upon me.

I was bound for the hell I deserved.

And then Jesus placed a stepstool in front of my cross and raised himself up to where he could reach my arms. With scissors, he cut the ropes from around my wrists and body and I fell into his arms, onto his body, even more ashamed now of my filthy condition. Then he carried me a short distance from the cross and laid me down on a pure white blanket, where he began bathing my naked body, lovingly and tenderly, as if every part of me was precious, just as I had washed my daughter when she'd been ill as a baby. The water he bathed me in glowed with light.

All the while, Jesus looked into my eyes with a deep knowing and an incredible depth of love and compassion. When he was finished, he cradled my head and offered me food for strength, and something to drink in a crystal chalice. I ate of the food because it seemed very important to him that I do so. Then he dressed me in a clean, white robe with a gold sash. All the while, he never said a word. Then I glanced to the side and saw, a short distance away, my parents lying next to each other, very still and either dead or in a coma. Their impact on my life was clear to me just then, and yet this moment with Jesus seemed so much more important. I heard myself saying, "Forgive them, Father; they did not know what they were doing."

I embraced Jesus, grateful not only for being alive, but for being deeply understood and loved. Then I found myself feeling slightly aroused, which caused a wave of guilt to wash over me, bringing the vision to an end. And then I was in my daughter's room again. She was still asleep and remained so while I sat on the floor for quite some time, unable to stop sobbing. Years later, in my journaling, I would think back to this moment and it brought to mind the time I'd wept after Dr. Mac had said that he could love me. But this feeling was even more intense. There would be times in the future when I would find myself tired of living, but I would never actively consider suicide again.

CHAPTER 17

JOURNEY

After the vision, my anxiety dissipated. I became more committed to my daily prayer discipline. I tried to reduce my drinking. After a few weeks, a couple members of the hospital staff asked me if I was pregnant again. No, I said. Why? Because you seem so calm and serene these days, they said. I hadn't been aware of any outside change in my behavior and it made me wonder what I must have seemed like before.

Even though I was less stressed, I still felt as if I needed guidance. The vision dissuaded me from thoughts of suicide, but where was I headed in the long run? *Where do I go from here?* I sought out the one person who knew me best, who knew me the longest. I decided to see Dr. Mac in Connecticut.

I caught Dr. Mac up to date with my marriage, the birth of Grace, and the death of Robin. I told him of my painful encounter with the psychologist who called me manipulative and narcissistic. And then I told him of my continued disappointment with my parents, how even the birth of their granddaughter didn't seem to bring us any closer.

Dr. Mac listened and then, in a kind tone, said, "Sarah, your parents are emotionally dead to you."

"But I can't live with dead parents!" I replied, shocked and hurt.

"Yes, you can," Dr. Mac said gently.

There was a lengthy silence as I tried to take in what Dr. Mac was saying to me. Surprisingly, I didn't cry. I just sat, dumbfound by the revelation. After a long while, Dr. Mac finally spoke again. "For whatever reason, Sarah, your parents are emotionally unavailable to you in any positive way. This is the way they are."

There was more silence, and then I told Dr. Mac of my emotional unraveling and of the subsequent vision experience. "What do you think it means?" I said. He agreed that it was powerful and asked if I was aware of the vision quest rituals of the Native American tribes. I told him I wasn't. "They consider visions like yours to be sacred, life-changing experiences," he said. "I might recommend you do some research about them at the library." This confirmed to me the importance of what had happened in my daughter's room that day. Thinking of Saint Paul's experience on the road to Damascus, I was not unfamiliar with the idea of life-changing visions, nor at all skeptical about them. My own experience was significant in some way, but how?

"What should I do about it?" I asked Dr. Mac. "It's a big responsibility."

"You need to work with it," he replied, "with the help of a local therapist. Perhaps a woman. Interview a few. Find one that you're comfortable relating to. Find one who shares your concerns about spiritual, as well as psychological, awareness and guidance." The idea of interviewing therapists had not occurred to me before.

Finally, I told Dr. Mac about my drinking and he said that I needed to find a way to stop. "The drinking won't help you," he said. "It can only hold you back." Then he told me of a book that had come out not long before entitled *The Relaxation Response* by Dr. Herbert Benson, a simple, secular introduction to transcendental meditation. Benson had done research demonstrating that meditation offered a positive way to deal with stress and he'd extracted the basic technique to make it accessible for everybody. Dr. Mac had a tape on the book's methodology and he gave it to me. As the time of our session came to an end, I thanked him for all his help over the years. My first appointment with him had been eighteen years prior. For most of that time, he had kept his hourly rate for me frozen at twenty-five dollars, a quarter of my weekly paycheck as an RN, even as his standard rate had eventually risen to sixty. Thinking back to our first time together, I mentioned that I didn't even know if I'd be able to make it into adulthood. He said he wasn't sure, either. He was surprised and delighted. He told me that I'd come so far, given the emotional turmoil of my family. He thought it was amazing that I had even been able to hold a job through all of it. I thanked him again for being such an anchor in my life, and he told me that his door would always be open.

Over the next few days, I listened to the tape Dr. Mac had given me. Meditation helped and I determined to learn more about it and practice it regularly. In the meantime, I began thinking heavily about what Dr. Mac had said about my parents. They were emotionally dead to me. Deep down I knew he was right. The problem was what to do about it. Cynthia called repeatedly, wondering when we were going to get together again. I kept turning her down with excuses until eventually she talked to my father about my obvious avoidance. My father responded by calling me, telling me he wanted us to have a loving family.

"Well, we have a problem with that," I told him. "And the problem is trust. I don't trust you at all. I don't trust you to be around my daughter, and I don't trust you to be around me." And then, instead of telling him that what he was asking for was never going to happen, I equivocated, still afraid of telling my father no. "I just really can't figure out how we can have a loving family," I said, as though the issue was something like a logistical problem. After I hung up the phone, I found myself repulsed by the idea of a loving family that would include my father.

That summer I attended a weekend retreat to pray and reflect about all that had happened. There, I was introduced to the Progoff Intensive Journal Program. This was a system of writing exercises to help you better connect with yourself, to gain more self-awareness and develop a better understanding of your life. The workshop was led by trained professionals, and there was a great respect for privacy. No nametags were handed out. I had been journaling off and on since my teens and the program appealed to me. Dr. Ira Progoff was a disciple of Carl Jung's, studying with him in Switzerland in the mid-1950s. From there, he further developed his theories of holistic depth psychology, the treatment of an individual that included the person's physical, mental, social, spiritual, and cultural life. It was a complete approach, fundamental and even life-altering. For Progoff, journaling was a big part of the process. The writing exercises were geared to help you look deeply into your life—your personal relationships, career, dreams (both sleeping and waking), and all the things that are meaningful to you. The idea was to explore pieces of your life without consciously thinking about them or judging them, thereby sparking further inner awareness. You'd write by allowing the words to flow on the page. There was no editing and no crossing out; only adding more explanation.

I found the journaling to be extraordinarily helpful. This was not the creation of a diary of events, like what I was used to. It was not the recording of where one's life had been. Rather, Progoff's journaling was concerned with the central question of where one's life was trying to go. Progoff had researched creativity and studied great artists, observing that they were able to look at their works as they were creating them and sense where the works were headed. It was about the art, never about the artist. What mattered most was what the art required. So it is, Progoff felt, with life itself. Journaling was a tool for one to be able to see one's life with the objectivity of a master artist, to discover clues as to where his or her life was trying to go, and the steps to be able to get there.

But first, when one begins writing, one uses the objectivity of an unbiased journalist. We were given workbooks and the first exercise was to write about where I was in my life in that period of time, what was happening, what potentially meaningful events had occurred. This was to include all aspects— work, health, relationships, culture, dreams, projects, and spirituality. I wrote about the vision experience, taking as detached a perspective as I could. The next step was called twilight imagery, where you sit silently, breathing, allowing your inner thoughts to process the piece you had just written, noting any imagery that might occur and jotting it down in a nonjudgmental way. This leads to additional thoughts and imagery, and you further journal with these in other exercises.

There were other parts to the journaling. There were dialogue exercises where you learn the process of dialoguing between yourself and somebody in your life, and you learn how to do so objectively. This could be somebody living or dead, since, as it was put in a way that I found very moving, death ends a life, but not a relationship. There was an exercise where you journal about the twelve "stepping stones" of your life. You start with your birth—everybody's first stepping stone—and you list the twelve major turning points that took you to where you now are. This is another means by which you can see where your life is trying to go. There was journaling about dreams. There was journaling about "wisdom figures"—people who come from faith traditions, authors, musicians, or anybody, living or dead, famous or obscure, who'd been influential in your life.

The final workshop exercise, called "Now, the open moment," is where you write about where you think your life is trying to go. I wrote about wanting to continue therapy. I wrote about participating in an incest survivor's group, an idea that had been in the back of my mind for a while, but only came to the forefront with the journaling. I wrote about making my home a more nurturing place. I wrote that the "healing of my most basic insecurities, fears, shame, isolation, seem to be taking place. I see my life more confident and joyful. Faithfulness, responsibilities, and attending to my family are crucial." In all the exercises, objectivity is the key. There is no judging, only reporting. And of course it's an ongoing process. I only scratched the surface during that weekend, but I came away with an awareness of how multifaceted everybody's life is. Despite my pain and struggle, I realized now that I was more than just a survivor of sexual abuse. I was more than my pain and loss. Where was my life trying to go? I would continue to follow the Progoff program for decades, ultimately amassing enough three-ring notebooks that I would contemplate someday writing this memoir.

I did a lot of reading, too. I wanted to learn more about the vision and I started studying the great religions of the world. As comforting as Jesus had been to me in the vision, I still found myself harboring anger at God. Why was there so much suffering in the world? I also read about sexual abuse. I read *I Never Told Anyone* by Ellen Bass, with writings by sexual abuse survivors, and *Father-Daughter Incest* by Judith Lewis Herman. Among other things, I learned that sexual abuse is often generational, and I wondered about my parents' childhoods, and why they spoke so little about their early years. Sometimes the reading was painful and I had to put the books down.

Finally, I started looking seriously for a therapist. The leader of the workshop had been a therapist at an interfaith center in Newton and I asked him if he could recommend a female therapist for me. He gave me a few names and I set about interviewing them as Dr. Mac had advised. I met with each of them. Along with their counseling experience with sexual abuse survivors, I wanted to know about their level of spirituality. I asked each one to tell me about their own spiritual journey. Some were taken aback by the question. Others talked about their church. One, a woman named Joan, said this: "My spiritual journey? That's what my whole life has been about." I liked her answer, but Joan was divorced and didn't have children and I wanted someone who had experience with motherhood and who could support me in my concerns about raising a child. This was important. I thought of the deficient role model that was my own mother, and I wondered what it was that made me think I could be a good mom to Grace. I was very aware of my own deficits and hoped a therapist could help me with my mothering.

There was a center in Cambridge, the Cambridge Women's Center, with support groups and resources for women. The center conducted a monthly drop-in survivor group. The center also had information about therapists who conducted survivor group meetings with a set number of participants in a time-limited, weekly group format of three or four months. I was barely ready for group as it was, let alone the drop-in groups, where different people, all strangers, would come and go. I inquired instead about the group experiences with the set number of participants but was told that, to be a member of one, you needed to be sober for at least a year and you needed to be active in therapy. I held off. I contacted a few more therapists, but, in the end, after praying for guidance, I came back to Joan. I couldn't forget her powerful answer to my question about spirituality. I still had some reservations, wondering if she'd be able to relate to my life as a mother. And I wanted to know she would believe me and that she understood the truth about incest. In one of my first sessions with her, I gave her a copy of *Father-Daughter Incest*. I knew discussing it would be helpful to me, and I asked her to read it. She promised she would.

Joan was in her early fifties, the same age as Casey Lynn, six years younger than my mother. Slightly taller than me at five-eight, she was an attractive woman with short, salt-and-pepper hair. She worked at a college counseling center in addition to her private practice. Joan had started out as an RN but went on to get her PhD in psychology, supporting herself the whole time. She was raised in Nova Scotia of Scottish descent, where her family attended a strict Calvinist church, but, as Joan got older, she sought her spirituality elsewhere, ultimately becoming a practicing Buddhist.

I would learn all this in time. To start, I had significant trust issues with Joan. I even took to tape recording our early sessions. This helped in another way; during the sessions, I was too anxious to process very much of the discussion and I learned a lot listening to the sessions later. During one of the sessions, I found myself having an anxiety attack. The fishhooks tore at my chest. I couldn't breathe and I ran out of Joan's office and down the stairs. She ran down the stairs after me, violating the boundaries of standard doctor/patient protocol.

"Sarah, where are you going?" she said as I rushed out of the building.

"Well, I can't sit in *there*," I answered, pointing back toward her office, trying to catch my breath.

"Okay," she said thoughtfully. "Well…what would dilute the situation?"

"Maybe we can just walk," I said. We walked. This was how our sessions evolved. Eventually, we'd end up walking to Boston Public Garden, where we'd sit and talk on a park bench amid the trees and flowers on the edge of the lagoon where the famous Victorian swan boats would silently glide by. Other times, we wouldn't sit at all. We'd just walk; I'd be too restless to do otherwise. I appreciated Joan's willingness to hold our sessions in this way, but I hadn't forgotten what Ryan had said and I wondered if maybe Joan, too, thought I was being narcissistic and manipulative. I asked her once if she was okay with our unconventional approach and she eased my mind when she said, "My office does not work for us; we need to do what works." Still, even with this, I felt anxious during our sessions. And vulnerable. But it was at least a comfort to me to know that, being outside, I could simply run away if I had to.

One time I told Joan that, when it came to discussing my incest, I was afraid she would not believe me. "Don't be ridiculous," she said. Her response infuriated me. My concern was very real. Indeed, it was one of the reasons I'd asked her to read Judith Lewis Herman's book. In *Father-Daughter Incest*, she documented how therapists often don't believe their clients. The next week, Joan apologized, telling me her approach was to remain centered as a therapist while taking seriously her clients' views and needs. She lost focus, she told me, and, with tears forming in her eyes, she said she understood my fears of not being believed. I was touched by her apology and told her we all make mistakes.

Looking back at my early anxieties with Joan, I can see other factors that aided and abetted them. I was probably afraid of getting into a shouting match, like I'd had with Ryan. And I might have even been afraid of a sexual advance, like my encounter with Casey Lynn. All in all, however, it wasn't so much Joan that made me anxious and vulnerable as it was the process itself. The process of healing. It was overwhelming and I was filled with trepidation. Was I even going about it in the right way? I continued journaling, "dialoguing" with Joan in my notebook. I prayed, too. I set up a small altar space where I would pray every morning. Sometimes I would imagine Jesus holding my hand in one hand and Joan's in the other. I'd ask for light and wisdom. I remained unsure of my path, but, through it all, I felt in some way as though I was at least making progress. The problem was that it was going to be a long journey. That was the only thing I knew for sure.

CHAPTER 18

JOAN

Two months into our sessions, I asked Joan if she'd read the copy I had given her of Judith Lewis Herman's *Father-Daughter Incest*. She admitted that she hadn't. I became angry with her and skipped a session and called her on the phone, telling her maybe we should take a break. She said if I wanted to, that would be all right. She understood, saying it was okay that I could make certain demands on her. She didn't find my request unreasonable, nor manipulative, which was important for me to hear. She'd agreed to read the book, after all. Finally, she read it, afterwards telling me she appreciated my bringing it to her attention, as well as my making demands. She said my standing up for myself was healthy.

Over the course of many sessions, we talked a lot about my trust issues. Joan understood my fears. I had told her about Ryan calling me narcissistic and manipulative and how that had hurt me. I didn't want to be hurt again. I told her that Ryan was young and I felt as if he didn't have enough life experience. Joan said, "What we are going to be doing in our work together is validating *your* experience." Nobody had ever said that before. She asked what it was that I thought fed into my inability to trust and I said that, if people knew who I really was, they'd be repulsed by me. "Don't you think they'd have compassion?" she asked. That hadn't occurred to me. I mentioned to her that my father had told me that I had made him do what he did to me. "And what's your sense of how your father manipulated *you?*" she asked. "He made you feel responsible." That hadn't occurred to me, either. Joan understood the dynamics of my family almost immediately, correctly identifying me as the family scapegoat and helping me see it. It was Joan who described our family as a solar system, with my father as the sun, and my mother and my sister and me as the orbiting planets. She asked me how I would feel if I could stand outside myself and hear my story. I told her I'd feel empathetic, and it started to dawn on me that maybe I was not as repulsive as I had imagined myself to be.

In fact, one of the goals Joan had with my therapy was for me to come to see that I did not have some kind of grotesque, underlying flaw, which, of course, I assumed I had. She also had me agree to a "contract," where, if I found myself again thinking seriously about suicide, I was to call her, no matter the time of day or night. She understood what it felt like to be suicidal. "We're in a place where we feel totally alone and without love" is how she described it. "An intolerable place for any of us to be." I told her that was how I felt—totally unloved. And unlovable. "And that's what causes the damage," she said.

We talked about my father, of course, and we talked about forgiveness. Because I'd wanted to be a good Christian, I had "forgiven" him back in my bedroom that day when he had asked for forgiveness for having been "a little fresh." Joan told me that forgiveness of deep pain can happen, but it has to be accompanied by an appreciation and understanding of what has happened and the impact of it on your life, otherwise what has happened becomes repressed. It requires acknowledging the anger and rage and sadness. In the process of healing from your wound, you increasingly become free of the power of the person who wounded you. Forgiving yourself for any resulting negative attitudes and behaviors is as important as letting go of the anger toward the one who has wounded you. Forgiveness, Joan told me, does not mean liking the person; it means letting go. True forgiveness cannot take place without these insights. Eventually, in the process of learning more positive attitudes and behaviors, scar tissue forms over our wounds. It is then possible to gradually let go of the pain, even though a scar remains.

After this, I asked Joan about Jesus's statement, about loving our enemies. To her understanding, it was about wanting good for them, as one would want good for any other person. It need not be an emotional feeling. Her explanation made me realize I had not forgiven my father. Or my mother. And I wondered if I ever could.

In the course of talking with Joan about my father's abuse, it suddenly seemed strange to me that, except for one brief mention, I had never discussed it with Dr. Mac in all the years I had seen him. I asked her about this. "As we develop more life experience and inner strength," Joan told me, "we're able to better cope. We have more emotional capacity to explore issues. You weren't ready back then. And the psyche is protective. You didn't have the mental resources at the time and so you unconsciously stopped yourself from going there." I knew she was right. I remembered back to those days and thought about how it seemed like a victory of sorts just to get through any given day.

I told Joan about my journaling, even reading some of my entries to her. She was familiar with the Progoff program, having gone through it herself. I talked to her about Pam, my friend who was also an incest survivor and who had attempted suicide. Pam ended up doing drugs. Her son would be put in foster care. I couldn't stop seeing myself in Pam, wondering if I was heading down the same road, while also feeling helpless about doing anything at all for Pam. Joan told me I needed to set boundaries. I needed to protect myself, she said. I couldn't take on the burdens of others.

On the first anniversary of my vision experience, I asked Joan what she thought it meant. She felt the vision was a process of knowing and feeling that I was loved, "an experience of unconditional love, something we all deeply long for."

At one point, Joan asked Tom to attend a session. She asked him how he was coping with my struggles. Tom said he was a traditional Catholic. His parents had actually separated twice, but they'd gotten back together both times. The marriage vows meant something—for better or for worse. Tom felt that the important thing was that I was working to try to get better. Tom asked Joan about the role of my spirituality. Joan said it was a valuable resource for me, so long as I wasn't using it to avoid difficult issues, imagining that God or Jesus would take care of everything without any effort of my own.

In truth, my spirituality was a critically important part of my healing. I joined an Episcopal healing prayer community at a local church that met every Friday. There were about twenty-five of us, every one of us broken in some way, either emotionally or physically. I felt safe there. There was a shared kindness among us. The priest celebrated the Eucharist. Then, if they wanted to, the group members would each go up to the altar with three or four others who would pray with them while the rest of the group sang modern hymns by Taizé, a Christian ecumenical monastic fraternity in France, as well as hymns by the monks of Weston Priory in Vermont, and other post-Vatican II musicians. These pieces were deeply moving and often times I would cry, dropping tears on the music pages as I was holding them. People would pray for each other as the music was being quietly sung and I found the whole experience very moving. Somewhere along the line, I came across Micah 6:8 and it helped me immensely: "And what does the Lord require of you? To act justly and to love mercy and to walk humbly with your God." That seemed manageable to me and it gave me some direction.

I asked Joan about her spirituality and she spoke about her journey, how she extricated herself from her strict Calvinist upbringing. Her father had been even stricter than the church. One Sunday the minister had talked about Hell as perhaps being a place of reform and repentance instead of a place of endless misery and torture. Joan's father had taken the family and walked out. When Joan got older, she sought another way.

Besides Joan, I rarely spoke to anybody about my past. I did, however, tell one friend about my sexual abuse—Rachael, the fellow nurse who was the art student. Rachael and I had become close as we coped with Robin's death. She struggled with her own issues. Her father had dropped dead from a heart attack when she was just seven. Her mother had been devastated and Rachael's childhood had been hard. She was working through her issues with art the way I'd been working through mine with journaling.

My overall anxiety persisted, however. I was still drinking heavily. My nightmares continued, too. In one recurring dream, I was all alone in an enormous cavern, holding a tall white candle that was so large I needed both hands to grasp it. I was walking along a narrow, sharply downward-sloping path, maybe no wider than a foot. It was pitch black in the cavern and I could not see below me, but I knew if I stepped off the path, or if the candle went out, I'd fall into a bottomless pit. The dream was terrifying and I'd wake up screaming.

At one point, Joan determined that I could benefit from antidepressant medication. I had refused medication before, concerned about how it might affect the baby if I became pregnant, but that window was closing and so now I agreed. Joan referred me to a psychiatrist who prescribed Prozac, which was relatively new at the time. I couldn't bring myself to go see him alone and so Joan walked with me to his office. In the office was an icon of the Blessed Mother holding the baby Jesus. It's the only thing I really remember about the visit. Mary was looking outward, with a countenance of deep compassion, even as she and her son were to endure such suffering.

It took about six weeks, but the Prozac began helping. I needed to stop drinking while on the medication and so I quit, the timing coinciding with the start of Lent that year. I went to a couple AA meetings, but the group was always predominantly men, and many of them reminded me just a little too much of my clients back at Boston City Hospital. Besides, for me, the core issue wasn't the alcohol. The core issue was the sexual abuse. My main reason to stop, besides the Prozac, was that I needed a year's sobriety to join the sexual abuse support group. But I gave it up for other reasons, too. I realized the drinking was a slow suicide and I also realized the pain and misery it could bring to Tom and Grace if I didn't find a way to stop.

About that time, I read M. Scott Peck's *The Road Less Traveled* and even went to one of his conferences. He talked about the Catholic Mass and about how one aspect of breaking the bread is to represent the idea that Jesus was accepting his brokenness, and nourishing us to help us accept ours as we grow in love of God, self, and neighbor. The idea resonated with me deeply. Joan gave me a strong piece of advice, too, for those moments when I would feel completely overwhelmed. "Think about what you can do, Sarah. What *can* you do? Can you go for a walk? Can you put on some music? Do what you *can* do."

Little by little, I began to discover other helpful resources. The priest to whom I had first confessed the incest, the one who had advised me to read the Genesis story of Joseph, had given gave me a booklet called *Responding to Incest: In Memory of Nancy*. Nancy was an incest survivor who had committed suicide. The booklet was written by Dr. Elaine Westerlund, who was the director of Incest Resources, a part of the Cambridge Women's Center, and an all-survivor, all-volunteer, nonprofit organization dedicated to supporting survivors of sexual abuse, the first such organization in the country. The booklet was a helpful read, but, more than anything, it made me aware that there were resources to be found. Therapy with Joan was helpful, but I could also do some digging on my own to acquire more specific knowledge.

Eventually, I started looking for the sexual abuse support group. This is where I was thinking it might be possible to heal. I would be with women survivors and learn from them. Therapy had been just a tool to get myself to the group. But, in my efforts to find one, I talked with a social worker, who told me I had it exactly wrong. "In my experience," she said, "the group is helpful and supportive. But the primary healing will come from your work with your therapist." This was disconcerting. I liked Joan, but I still had trust issues. I still hadn't gotten past my experience with Ryan. I couldn't imagine one-on-one therapy being the answer.

I said as much to Joan once, who said, "Sarah, have you consciously decided never to trust anyone ever again?" I hadn't thought of it that way. I hadn't actually thought of it as a conscious choice I was making. Around that time, I saw a PBS special on the author and motivational speaker Leo Buscaglia, or "Dr. Love," as he was known. I read his book, *Living, Loving, and Learning*. Buscaglia said, in life, we had to choose between love and fear. For me, the main factor was trust; I could choose love and trust, or fear and distrust. And I knew on some level that fear and distrust would lead me to loneliness, pain, and madness.

I talked more to Joan about Ryan. She disagreed with his perception of me as narcissistic and manipulative. Manipulative clients are always looking for someone else to blame, Joan said. They often hold their therapists responsible. I was not that way, Joan assured me. "It sounds to me," she said, "as if Ryan didn't have a lot of life experience; he hadn't suffered great loss in his life." Then she smiled and said, "I'm smarter than he is, Sarah."

I mentioned Rachael to Joan one time and, knowing that I put trust in Rachael, she suggested we all meet. Rachael could give me an objective view. Rachael agreed and her and I decided to meet Joan at the Ritz Carlson, right across from Boston Garden, for formal tea. After tea, Rachael told me she thought Joan was genuine and was looking out for my best interests. I was continually surprised at how willing Joan was to work with me outside of the standard protocols. In order to reach me, she knew she had to. Still, she could have dismissed me altogether. That she didn't was something I would come to appreciate more and more as time went along.

One time Rachael introduced me to a kind of art therapy, where you have a plaster mask of your face created to represent you and your feelings about yourself. The person making the mask uses the same kind of rolled-up plaster used to make a cast. The person having the mask made lies down while the other takes lengths of the plaster, warmed with hot water, and presses it gently around the first person's face and neck to make the impression. You breathe through a straw while this is being done to you, which, for me, took a great amount of trust. I made Rachael's mask and she made mine. The plaster was white, the only color they had back then. We made our masks in Rachael's apartment and I asked her for the blackest black paint she had and she pulled out something called Mars black, named for the Roman god of war. My white mask started as a blank canvas, but, after I painted it, it looked like dark charcoal, a blackness that no light could enter or reflect from. The mask—my face—looked as if it had been charred in a fire. To me, it was the hell I'd been living. Rachael was so unnerved by it that, when it dried, she had to cover it with a towel. I came back a week later intending to paint the inside and I wanted black for that, as well. But when we went to look for the tube of Mars black, it was gone. Rachael and I turned her apartment upside down, but the paint was nowhere to be found and the inside of the mask remained the original plaster white.

I decided I needed Joan to see the mask. And yet I felt extraordinarily vulnerable doing so. It would be showing Joan who I was and how I felt in a way I had never come close to doing before. I couldn't bring the mask to her office, or show it to her in Boston Public Garden. I was afraid of her reaction and I needed a secure place. I asked her to join me in the safe environment of the Church of the Advent, the church where Tom and I were married, just a couple blocks from the Garden. We walked there during one of my usual appointments. I asked permission from the church secretary for access to the sanctuary. As we entered, Joan asked me what going into a church meant to me. I told her it represented 2,000 years of spiritual truth, and prayers in every season of a person's life, and holiness, and something much larger than my small life. Joan and I sat side by side in a pew and I had the mask wrapped up in a Budweiser beach towel. Pulling it out from the canvas bag I'd carried it in, I described the process of making it and how I had used the Mars black and how I had wanted to paint the inside black, too. She listened to me respectfully and looked upon the mask. Then she said she had some sense of the depth of my pain. She appreciated the positive ways I was trying to work through it and she said she'd support me in my journey. She also said that maybe an angel had taken the missing black paint to purposely leave the inside of it the original plaster white. The universe meant for it to be so.

I had now opened myself completely to Joan and she hadn't recoiled or criticized me. She hadn't left. She wasn't going to leave. I didn't have to go it alone. And, in that moment, I decided I was going to do something I couldn't do before. I decided I was going to trust.

CHAPTER 19

LOSS AND TRANSFORMATION

Daily I had to practice choosing love and trust. Often, I'd fail. I still had anxiety attacks. In the age before cell phones, if Tom came home late, I'd imagine the worst. I'd be certain something terrible had befallen him. It would be my fault, of course. I hadn't been worthy of him in the first place.

As a way to cope with my concerns, I would journal every morning after getting Grace off to school on the kindergarten bus. I'd give myself a half hour to journal about everything I might have been obsessing about, then I'd close the book and move on with my day. I'd make a to-do list to help me stay focused. About that time, I read an article in *Reader's Digest* called "Lessons from Aunt Grace," by Nardi Reeder Campion. Campion had been going through loss in her life when she came upon her Aunt Grace's diary. Aunt Grace, too, had gone through loss, losing her sweetheart in the Spanish-American War. To keep herself together, she resolved to do six things per day. Those things were to do something for herself, do something for someone else, do something you don't want to do but that needed doing, do a physical exercise, do a mental exercise, and say an original prayer that always includes counting her blessings.

This modest list seemed realistic to me and I resolved to follow it. I was not always faithful, especially about doing chores I didn't want to do, but my daily attempts provided me with a routine and helped address Joan's idea about doing what you *can* do. Sometimes doing something for myself could be an activity as simple as having a cup of tea or reading a book, or maybe taking a walk, which would double as physical exercise. Doing the original prayer came easy to me, although many times it was no more than a quiet mantra—"Please, God, help me"—that I'd invoke whenever I started feeling a panic attack coming on. I placed little angels in every room of the house, and a "Smile, God loves you" coffee mug on the kitchen windowsill, where I would be certain to see it. And then I'd make it a point to smile.

I thought of the coincidence of the name, Aunt Grace and my Grace. Maybe the name is what attracted me to read the article in the first place, as if my daughter somehow led me to it. My desire to be a good mother was part of my healing, after all. I thought of Isaiah 11:6: *And a little child shall lead them.*

I maintained my friendship with Rachael, whom I appreciated for several reasons, not least of which was her belief that my vision meant something significant. She'd experienced something similar herself. It was a dream of her late father. She was in high school when she'd had the dream, at a time when she came to fully realize that her father would not be there to see her graduate. She suddenly understood that he wouldn't be there to walk her down the aisle at her wedding, to see his potential grandchildren, or to share in any of her life's milestones. The sudden comprehension of this was heartbreaking for her and she found herself essentially grieving for her father a second time. In the dream, she met him in a garden. They shared an ice cream and walked and talked and spent a wonderful afternoon together. When the day came to a close, Rachael's father told her their paths were going to separate. He drew a diagram showing that she would have to walk a half circle one direction while he'd have to walk a half circle in the other direction. But eventually, their paths would meet at the other end of the circle. Rachael told me that, since that dream, although she'd felt sadness, she never felt the same level of despair.

Rachael talked to me of a spiritual mentor who told her we should think of our lives as the life of Christ. We all suffer loss, as Christ suffered a death on the cross, but after a loss comes transformation, as with Christ's resurrection. It's our life's work to make something positive out of our loss. Loss must not define us, causing bitterness or destructive behaviors. Loss must never win. Rachael's favorite saying was an old Spanish proverb and it perfectly captured this idea: *Living well is the best revenge.* She put the saying in calligraphy on a four-by-six card and gave it to me, framed. I have it still, resting on my bookcase.

I told Joan about Rachael's dream and she felt it was powerful. We talked about how, despite her father's death, Rachael still had his love, something I never had from my own, living father. Joan, even though a Buddhist, believed in Christ's suffering and resurrection because she said that life was ultimately stronger than death. She felt we were all the body of Christ because we all suffer. And, as we struggle and grow—and become increasingly whole—so Christ becomes increasingly whole. And then we can offer ourselves to the world, as Christ offers himself to the world. Buddhists, Joan told me, believe that life is suffering. But it is so because of what Buddhists refer to as impermanence. There is always loss because all things change, and if we do not understand this, and if we do not understand that loss itself ultimately becomes transformed, then we create our own suffering. We compound this by errantly attaching ourselves to that which is destined to perish or change or is simply unimportant. I came to realize that I was creating some of my own suffering by attaching myself to the idea that I could change things that were out of my control. Of course, by then I'd been introduced to the idea of meditation, a staple of Buddhist practice, and around that time I read Jon Kabat-Zinn's book, *Wherever You Go, There You Are*, a book about mindfulness and being in the moment. I didn't really know of an equivalent concept of "the moment" in Christianity. I worked on being in the moment, on letting go of the troubles of the past and the worries of the future.

In one visit with Joan, she asked if I trusted God and I had to admit that, no, even with all my spiritual seeking and even with the vision, I did not entirely trust God. Suggesting why that might be so, she then asked me how much I was able to separate God the Father from my father. It was an especially astute question. The Church had always seemed patriarchal to me and it was hard to break away from the thought of God as a male parent. I could never forget having to sing "This Is My Father's World" in church as a little girl. Joan also asked me how well I was able to separate suffering from being "punished" by God. "Do you love God?" she asked me at one point. I answered that I did, but I knew I was burdened with flaws and inadequacies and I feared what might happen to me if God changed his mind about me and my love would go unreturned. She asked if I prayed about my fears and sadness. I said no, and that, instead, I prayed for others. Praying for others was always important to me. Besides, why would God care about me? To which Joan reminded me of the parable of the shepherd leaving the ninety-nine sheep to go in search of the single lost one. She would also remind me of the passage that "not a sparrow falls without God's knowledge." At one point, we talked about how I didn't feel worthy of anything I had, that I didn't deserve a husband like Tom or a daughter like Grace. Joan asked me how I imagined life might be different if I felt deserving. I didn't have an answer. Joan continually gave me food for thought.

She talked about emotions and how we need to be aware of what triggers them. When we're children we think that our emotions come from outside of us. The outside world makes us angry or frustrated or depressed. Part of the growth process is to see that anger and frustration and depression all come from within us. With this awareness, we can find more productive ways of coping. We did a lot of work with cognitive behavioral therapy for me to identify and cope with my triggers.

I found myself in disagreement with Joan on one point. I told her during one session that I thought it was a miracle I was still alive. "That's just your belief system," she told me. I'd been suicidal on and off since my teens and, at one point, was saved from killing myself by an astonishing vision. "How can you say it's not a miracle that I'm alive?" I said. It was the first time I'd asked Joan a question for which *she* didn't have an answer.

In the meantime, I continued to work on the mask. I placed a rosary on it, encircling the face, with the crucifix over the larynx, thus signifying that my voice had been silenced. The rosary was a pearl rosary and I liked the symbolism of the pearls, the way an oyster suffers but then creates something of beauty. And it was the rosary I used when saying rosaries for Robin. I used Elmer's glue to create tears running from the eyes and down the cheeks. I placed a small, red fabric heart below the mask and I ran a paring knife through it, then decided the knife came out too easily, so I embedded the heart with fish hooks, symbolizing the pain it would take to pull them out. I wrapped the mask in Saran Wrap, as if it was being suffocated. The Saran Wrap also represented my unseen isolation from others. I placed the mask on the Budweiser towel to represent the drinking I had used to cope with all that the mask symbolized. The mask was the perfect embodiment of how I had felt my whole life.

Eventually, I decided I needed to go beyond the notes I had been writing in my journal to myself. I needed to write to others. Specifically, I needed to make my feelings known in writing to my mother, my sister, my grandmother, and my Aunt Iris. The letters were all similar in detailing the history of the abuse, but the one to my mother was much more pointed. I sent it along with the unopened presents she had sent us that past Christmas. Opening presents should be an experience of joy, I wrote, explaining that I felt no joy from her. I had written her earlier that fall, asking her to join me in a session with Joan about our relationship, where we might be able to better communicate, without assigning blame. "Can't we have a relationship without demands?" she wrote back. I brought this up in the letter, the idea that seeking a more meaningful relationship with her daughter was a "demand." I wrote that her constant digs, always couched in subtlety but with a clear streak of dark meanness, made me feel like I had been beaten up by her black velvet gloves. "I am convinced that your constant favoritism of Brenda, and coldness, and criticism, and emotional neglect of me were instrumental in allowing Dad to commit, and perpetrate, his evil acts. You allowed the incest to happen." I reminded her of when she'd walked in on my father and me in their bed. I reminded her of the time in the car, when my father admitted to my mother that he had been "a little fresh with me." She had mentioned divorce to him, but never took the time to ask me what he had done to me. I reminded her of the suicide attempts, and about how she had sat silently in the psychiatrist's office in Albany when my father said if I wanted to commit suicide, he would do nothing to stop me. I reminded her of not visiting when Grace was born. I reminded her about the engagement ring she'd talked my grandmother into giving to her. I told her I had learned that incest runs in families and I wondered if she was a survivor, too. Finally, I told her that, unless we could talk together with my therapist, there would be no further dialogue between us, and signed the letter "Sincerely."

I sent the letters out in January of 1987. In sending them, I felt as though I was owning my truth, no matter the consequences. Aunt Iris responded sympathetically, saying she was very sorry to hear about all that had happened. My grandmother called and told me my mother loved me and then asked rhetorically, "What could your mother have done?" To her credit, she said she called my mother and told her the ring would now be left to me. Then again, Aunt Iris had already told me she had spoken to my grandmother; it was really Aunt Iris's idea to leave the ring to me.

My grandmother said she was surprised to hear of the suicide attempts, but said I now needed to "give my bitterness to the Lord." She also asked me why, if things had been as I said, that I had invited my father to my wedding. I couldn't explain to her my desperate need for normalcy at that time. Later, I would come to understand how prevalent my grandmother's kind of thinking is, the denial and the deflection.

Brenda called and said I shouldn't have sent the letter to our grandmother because it upset her. Then she tried to assure me that "Mom loves you," adding that she hoped I hadn't sent an angry letter to Dad. "He'd probably kill you," she said. I didn't believe she was exaggerating, which is why I had, in fact, not sent a letter to our father.

To my partial surprise, my mother wrote back. "I was genuinely upset when I read your letter. Before we can do anything to reconcile our differences, I am going to talk to your psychologist. Please send me her phone number. I have always loved you and still do." She signed it, "Love, Mother." It was typical. Now that her family knew she'd initially refused to talk with Joan, she couldn't bear the thought of looking like the bad guy. I talked to Joan about it. She confirmed in my mind that it was unlikely my mother would change her behavior. Her motivation was to save face. Most likely, she'd spend the session trying to turn things around and point blame back at me. Nevertheless, I sent her Joan's number. But I told her it was no longer necessary to call, giving her an out, which she happily took. I've never heard from her since.

CHAPTER 20

GROUP

In late April of 1987, I started group therapy with an almost suffocating amount of trepidation. It was to run through August. Having Joan to talk to during that time period became more important than ever. Knowing I was going into the incest survivors group, I had asked Joan if she was planning any vacations or time off. It was imperative that she be available to me. She'd assured me she'd be there for me, but right before group was set to begin, she told me that, during the summer, she'd be traveling for a week to California for a conference related to a new position she was taking at the college where she worked.

I took it as a betrayal. I was angry and bitter. I sent Joan a long letter telling her I wanted to take a leave of absence from our therapy. I told her that her not being available to me for a week during one of the most anxious times of my life was tantamount to breaking our contract. I reminded her of my fear of abandonment, about my shame and how afraid I was of people discovering that I was filthy and disgusting, and then leaving me. And now she was leaving. Yes, it was only for a week, but, in my mind, weeks during group therapy were sure to feel like months.

Joan replied with a very thoughtful, heartfelt letter, starting out by reminding me that the Chinese character for crisis also means opportunity. "We have a crisis," she wrote. "I hope we can turn it into an opportunity." Her new position, she explained, was as International Student Advisor and the conference was required for her to learn her new responsibilities, which were to include acting in the interests of students who were far from home and on foreign soil. The week was not a vacation for her. In fact, the conference was mandatory. She said she understood my concerns, my feelings, my fears. She knew of my abandonment issues and how, to me, her actions represented "a repeat of numerous family situations." But she hadn't known about the conference when she had told me she wasn't going anywhere. She asked me to trust her heart, saying that she trusted mine—"a large, loving heart that rises from the Heart of life and gives freely to others." The letter continued: "I also think there exists a painfully isolated Cinderella who thinks she is only a chimney sweep; who doesn't know that she owns a glass slipper and the Prince (of Peace) looks everywhere for her."

Nevertheless, I stopped seeing Joan. I couldn't stop believing that the weeklong trip was her subtle means of backing away from me. I was certain she wanted out.

In the meantime, to cope with my seemingly never-ending anxiety, I frequently found myself tempted to drink. But my fear was that, if I ever again attempted suicide, it would probably be while I was drunk, and this was enough to dissuade me, at least most of the time. I had another way of keeping the thoughts at bay, too. I would often visualize Grace, now five years old, having to gaze upon my lifeless body, resting in its casket at my funeral. Grace would hold my death as a memory for her whole life, just as Rachael had remembered her father's death when she was just seven.

With Joan, we'd discussed many times my lack of self-worth. I wasn't interested in staying alive for myself. I wasn't important to myself. But I was important to my daughter. I loved so many things that went along with being a mother. I loved doing all of the things with Grace that my mother had never done with me. Starting when she was a baby, we read together, which became part of her night-time ritual. We said prayers before bed and then I would kiss her on the forehead goodnight. On my days off, we watched Sesame Street and Mister Rogers, whose calm, kind, thoughtful demeanor probably meant more to me than it meant to Grace. I loved his song, "It's You I Like," and, depending on the day, sometimes it would make me tear up. I always tried to listen to Grace, who would tell me about her day. Tom and I supported her interests. There was no spanking or hitting. Discipline was about learning lessons, consequences, and the use of a timeout chair. All of this, engaging with my daughter in a way my mother never engaged with me, was immensely healing. Knowing I was important to Grace gave me strength.

And I knew I was important to my patients, too. This was all enough for me to want to keep living, and that aided my attempts to remain sober. In the meantime, I maintained my daily "to-do" list from the "Lessons from Aunt Grace" piece I'd read in *Reader's Digest*. I knew it wasn't enough to say no to the alcohol; I needed things to say yes to. Along with that, I would say my short, repetitive prayer: *Please, God, help me; what do you want me to do?*

The group started meeting in late April. There were five of us and there would be sixteen two-hour sessions moderated by two social workers. Everyone came from incredibly broken and dysfunctional families. This was something of an epiphany for me. For some reason, I had assumed I was the only person to have come from such a family. On the one hand, it was somewhat reassuring to know there were others. On the other hand, I quickly came to see that nobody was going to have the answers I was looking for. Nobody was any further ahead than I was. We were all in the same tragic boat. As far as I could tell, there was going to be enormous grief involved in the process.

The abuse stories each member had were similar and yet each one unique. Relating them was the overall goal of the group. We would each be given forty-five minutes to an hour to tell our stories to the group without interruption. None of us had ever told our entire stories before. We might have confided little pieces here and there to friends or family members, but we'd all kept secret the full details. I decided that I'd read my story, afraid that I would never be able to just speak it to the group. I began a separate journal to write out exactly what I would ultimately say.

But all that was down the road. The first sessions were just about getting to know each other. The sessions would open with a "check-in," where we'd each say how we were doing. Each person would take five minutes or so. If you had something you wanted to further discuss, maybe an incident that day or week that had triggered some sort of emotional crisis, you mentioned it here and then, after check-in, the group would circle back around to it. Check-in often helped establish the agenda for the balance of the session.

I brought up my issues with Joan to the group. I couldn't hold back my rage as I spoke about the betrayal I had perceived. A couple of the others mentioned that their therapists were going on vacation, and such was my level of distortion that I found myself stunned that they weren't bothered by that. One of the members, "Donna," reacted hostilely, upset that I was bringing such anger into the room, saying, "I don't have to take care of her!" I shut down, like a deer in headlights. Later, I talked privately to Shirley, one of the social workers. She said that Donna had reacted that way because I had activated in Donna her own suppressed anger. This made sense and I felt some relief. By then, I was getting more and more to the point where I realized I could no longer spend my time trying to please other people. That and pretending to be happy were two behaviors I could no longer engage in.

I told Shirley I was hoping she could become my new therapist. I explained to her my belief that Joan was looking for a way to abandon me. Maybe she'd even been doing it unconsciously, I reasoned. I told Shirley that I'd chosen that particular time of the year to engage in group because Joan had originally assured me that she'd be around. Otherwise, I would have waited for the fall group sessions. I felt manipulated.

Shirley told me my anger was understandable. I told Shirley of my history with Ryan and she said it was amazing I was able to have any kind of trusting relationship with a therapist. Then she said, "Sarah, your relationship with Joan must be very important to you. Otherwise, you wouldn't be so upset." Then she offered to call Joan, to talk to her and get a more objective viewpoint. She came back to me after doing so and told me she thought that Joan was a good therapist for me. Joan seemed to her to be very sensitive to issues of incest survival. Shirley didn't find any reason why Joan would have made any conscious or unconscious act to terminate our therapy. No history of abuse in her own life, for example. Then Shirley said she wouldn't be my therapist because she didn't want to rob me of the experience of working through my disappointment and anger with Joan. Doing so would give me the opportunity to confront a major crisis and come through it in a growing, positive way.

I wasn't convinced. I needed further guidance and I drove down to Connecticut to see Dr. Mac. We'd kept in touch. He had called me a year before to tell me that Brig had passed away at the age of eighty-six. We'd been on vacation during the funeral, but, when we returned, I traveled to Naugatuck to put red geraniums on Brig's grave, red being Brig's favorite color, and I said a prayer of gratitude.

When I arrived that evening in Dr. Mac's office, I explained about Joan. I told him how depressed and anxious I'd been. I had even had thoughts of suicide again. "Sarah," he said, "if you commit suicide, your daughter has a three-hundred-percent greater chance of committing suicide." This was a sobering statistic. Nevertheless, I felt lost, and I told him how betrayed I'd felt by Joan's apparent abandonment of me. For once, Dr. Mac did not seem to understand me. He laughed, in fact, at my concern, which made me furious. I told him so. "Well, that's too damn bad," he said. I picked up my pocketbook, walked out, and drove the two hours back to Boston.

To this day, I'm not sure why Dr. Mac said what he said that evening. Was it tough-love? If it was, I was not ready for it. I felt betrayed once again. On the other hand, Dr. Mac's apparent indifference to my feelings made me more aware of how seriously Joan had taken them, as evidenced by the things she'd said in her letter.

Back in group, the stories eventually came out. "Donna" had been abused by her father. Donna was thirty-four, petite, blond, and pretty. Her father had died in a mental hospital when she was seventeen. Her mother was still alive, a sixty-eight-year-old active alcoholic who was living with her seventy-eight-year-old boyfriend. Just a few months before, the boyfriend had French-kissed Donna. She had only recently recalled her father's sexual abuse, having repressed it more or less her entire life. Now that she was aware of it, she felt she could be healed, as if awareness was the entire key. Of course I thought so, too, but we would both discover that healing was never so simple. In Donna's case, her suppression had manifested itself in chronic depression and a breakdown. She was on disability. She couldn't drive. She had trouble eating and sleeping. For most of her life, she was easy prey for men. If a man showed her any affection, she told us, "I was his." Donna had recently taken to nailing her apartment windows shut to feel more safe and a few times she came to the sessions with a teddy bear. She was also in the process of legally changing her name, rejecting outright her birth name.

"Judith" was short with dark brown hair. She had a responsible job in a bank, but she admitted she was underemployed for her education and abilities. Her abuse came at the hands of a family friend, her father's drinking buddy. He'd come over to their house on Saturdays and drink beer and begin roughhousing with Judith, his hands ultimately going into her pants. Her father would watch and laugh, sometimes chuckling that Judith was getting "what she deserved." He repeated this one day when she ultimately confronted her whole family about the abuse. "You never got anything you didn't deserve." Relating this experience to us, she said, "I have to hear from the group that I didn't deserve it." Of course she didn't, we all told her.

Judith saw herself as the maverick of the family, trying hard to be who she wanted to be. To her, it seemed as though her father encouraged his friend's abuse as a means by which to break Judith like a horse. The friend came along with the family to the beach one day when Judith was twelve and the roughhousing started up again. This time the mother was present but did nothing. The friend let Judith go only after her siblings had pleaded for him to stop. Judith told us her mother was a "doormat" and a heavy drinker. Judith became anorexic in high school, even hospitalized for it at one point. She told us that she'd learned that a high percentage of anorexics have a history of sexual abuse. For Judith, it was a problem with balance. She would either feel undeserving and go without, or she would overindulge, whether it was food or sex. But she proclaimed to us that now that she understood her abuse, she could be healed.

"Patricia" was in her late twenties and very sweet. She'd been abused by an uncle from the age of five. Patricia was the youngest of four daughters and all of them had been abused by the same uncle. It would start with tickling and progress from there. Two of the sisters, at the ages of twelve and sixteen respectively, had simultaneously approached their mother about the abuse, but she hadn't believed them. Years later, after the uncle died, their mother did, finally, allow for the idea that sexual abuse might have taken place at his hands. But she claimed that if she had known about it at the time, she would have stopped it. As I listened to Patricia tell this to the group, I wondered what more her mother had needed to hear besides the pleas for help from those two daughters.

Incredibly, "Linda," the sixteen-year-old sister, now fully grown and with children of her own, had admitted once to Patricia that, if Linda's own son told her he'd been abused, Linda probably wouldn't believe him either, thus perpetuating their mother's denial of a phenomenon that Linda, herself, had experienced firsthand. Such is the power of wanting to remain insulated from hideous truths. In fact, none of the sisters besides Patricia had ever wanted to talk about their own abuse, all of them believing they'd somehow moved on, and all of them believing it ridiculous that Patricia could not do the same. She was in the group talking to strangers because she could not share her victimhood with those closest to her—who had survived the exact same experience of abuse.

I would think about this later and come to understand how powerful the pull of family must be to deny sexual abuse. The acknowledgement of its presence would not be survivable for a family. Only with its denial can a family remain intact, and there are those who are willing to pay that cost. This is the secret, painful dynamic in families where sexual abuse is present. And in its essence, that was the point of the group, to talk about the secrets that nobody had ever dared talk about.

"Cheryl" was a thirty-seven-year-old single woman who worked with handicapped children. She was attractive and always nicely dressed, but she told us she felt as though she was pretending at life. If people really knew her, they'd see how needy she was, she told us. All she wanted was to be held. Her mother was a prescription pill addict. Her father was a CPA and had spent Cheryl's childhood more or less unavailable to her. Cheryl's abuser was her piano teacher, a friend of the family. She was only five when the abuse started. She would go to the piano teacher's house and he would put his penis in her mouth and put flutes and other instruments in her vagina. For three years this went on. During this time, her mother was busy attending to Cheryl's cancer-stricken older brother, who would die at the age of ten, creating almost impossible family dysfunction. When Cheryl told her mother that she didn't want to continue taking lessons, her mother became angry. Like the rest of us, Cheryl had nobody to confide in. She tried telling her sister, but then felt guilty for doing so. Eventually, she tried to forget the abuse. In high school, on her very first date, Cheryl was raped. She didn't start getting her periods until she was twenty-one. She was now suffering with endometriosis. Much later in life, Cheryl talked to her mother about the piano teacher and her mother denied not only the abuse but also that Cheryl had ever taken piano lessons.

Quickly, I began to see a common theme—mothers who, for whatever reason, were unavailable to their children, refusing to help or even acknowledge the abuse, often right under their own roofs. Mothers who enabled the sexual abuse. Another common theme was the self-blame. Cheryl still felt shame from not somehow doing more to stop her abuse, even though she was only five when it began. I was the only mother in the group, and I happened to have a five-year-old. This allowed me to add some perspective. "My five year old is so innocent and trusting," I said. "Like any five year old, she'd do anything to please her parents or trusted adults. And she trusts implicitly. You can't ask anything else of a child that age. You couldn't have stopped it. It wasn't your fault."

I started seeing Joan again shortly after her return. After all, Shirley had said she was all right. I had called Joan after her letter, before she'd left for her conference, and I had sworn at her and told her I was sure she was setting me up, "just like my mother." I said ugly things. Joan spoke calmly and rationally to me, and, later in life, thinking back to these days, I would find myself in awe of Joan's composure and patience.

At the time, I started wearing all black to our sessions. I wore a rosary around my neck, too, and I often brought along my mask. I'd see Joan twice a week and we'd meet in her office and walk to the Church of the Advent, the only place I felt safe. During one session, I carved a smiley face onto the back of the heart with a razor to symbolize Dr. Mac's laughing at me. In my first session back, Joan told me she thought it was important for me to have the experience of being angry at someone and yet be able to find a way to salvage the relationship. This was an entirely new process to me. Being angry with someone didn't mean you had to leave them. And it also didn't mean they'd abandon you or abuse you, two things I had, of course, always feared. There had always been only these two outcomes in my mind. Abuse, like my father, or emotional abandonment, like my mother. I apologized to Joan. We worked on my not being so controlled by my pain. "You're on an emotional seesaw," Joan said, "with the mask on one end, representing pain and betrayal. The other side is your goodness and spirituality." She drew it as a diagram, writing underneath the diagram, *Who is Sarah?* "What's missing," she said, "is a core where you can hold the mask as part of your experience without allowing it to control you." Developing that core, the center of that seesaw, became the major focus of our work.

One night at the group, I brought in my mask. I said a prayer for strength. Everyone commented on the black exterior and the white interior of the mask. "Better than white outside with blackness on the inside," Donna said. "Like your father." By then, Donna had told me she realized that getting upset with me earlier was her issue, not mine.

After I showed the mask, everyone wanted to hear my story, but I was still reluctant. In fact, I would be the last one to tell it. Working up to it over the weeks, and writing in my journal about it, I found myself often feeling nauseous. During the course of the group therapy, I lost my appetite, along with twelve pounds. It took me until almost the end of the group before I could relate the details of my father's abuse. Even then, I was close to a panic attack. It surprised me how hard it was to talk about my experiences to these people, even though they had told me about their own abuses. To work up some strength, I introduced meditation and prayer into the group, which everyone went along with. In fact, over the course of the sessions, I had talked openly about my spirituality. Before I told my story, I recited a prayer for blessings, guidance, and peace.

What we all suffered from in telling our stories was the enormous shame, grief, disgust, and confusion we felt about our abuses. At one point, I realized that having sex with my father was the only thing that had pleased anyone in my family. Upon that realization, I cried for the little girl that I once was.

We'd also lived our lives in fear of not being believed. This was a hard thing to overcome. We talked a lot about trust—when to trust and how much or how little to trust. None of us were well-versed in asking for help, either. Once, Cheryl skipped out of a Friday session and I called her at home to check on her. "Are you okay?" I asked. She said she wasn't. She'd had a terrible week and was just trying to get through each day. The thought of group was too overwhelming. But she was touched that somebody thought to call. It hadn't occurred to her that others might care enough to reach out to her. Help was available to her, but this was a completely new idea to her. Little by little, through our fellow group members, we each began to see the distortions in our own thinking.

As with Cheryl, we all needed to be there for each other. Oftentimes, the obligation I began to feel for the others was the only thing that motivated me to attend the sessions. I was overcome with a sense of needing to be present and to listen to these survivors. In the back of my mind was the terrible thought of someone showing up for the group one night, especially ready to tell their story, and nobody else being there.

My own fear of telling was exacerbated at one point during my time in group therapy by a visit to a chiropractor for my chronic neck and back pain. I had been diagnosed with arthritis in my neck in my twenties. I mentioned my abuse to the chiropractor. Later in the session, while I was lying on the table, with her working my back, she mentioned that she knew of a therapy that included the insertion of the therapist's gloved finger into a client's rectum to bring back memories. She offered to do it. I rose from the chiropractor's table, put my clothes on, and walked out. I talked about the experience in group and was applauded for walking out. One of the social workers said I'd absolutely done the right thing, calling the chiropractor's offer "totally inappropriate." Any time you're with a professional in a closed setting such as that, she elaborated, you're in a position that is exceedingly vulnerable, similar to the environment of the abuse. Interestingly, Cheryl said that she wondered if she would have had the strength to walk out as I did, and it struck me how truly worn-down a victim can become.

At one point, it was suggested that we role-play, with one person playing the sexual abuse perpetrator and the other playing the victim. I could not do it. I watched as two of the others started the role play and had an anxiety attack, almost fainting. I had been prone to these. My PTSD was triggered easily, and still is to this day. I startle easily. I'm the

172

person who involuntarily screams when someone accidentally drops a plate in a restaurant or a car backfires on the street. And it always takes a while for me to regain my composure. That day in the group, they stopped the role-play, and one of the social workers attended to me with a cold washcloth while other members of the group suggested I pray or meditate to calm myself.

Around this time, I received a box from my father. Years earlier, when he'd sold our home, he had gotten rid of all of my things, or so I had been told. Now, out of the blue, he sent me a box of some of my belongings from childhood. I couldn't imagine him taking the time and I wondered if he sent the box at his wife's insistence. There were a couple of my Bibles, including the Bible I had read with my grandfather with the underlined verses that we had discussed when he was warning me about going to hell. There were some keepsakes from the sailing camp, too. And then there were some Easter dresses my mother had made, along with the orange dress she had made for my dance recital. I cried seeing myself as the little girl who had worn those dresses. And then I thought of how creepy it was that my father had held on to them all these years. I knew exactly what that little girl had meant to him.

Meanwhile, the Thursday night group therapy continued. We talked about our pain and loss and fear and shame and guilt and isolation. I felt overwhelmed with compassion for the others. On Friday nights, I'd go to the healing prayer group at church. I marveled at the scheduling—the survivors group on Thursdays and the healing prayer group the very next night. *How gracefully timed*, I thought. The healing prayer group became an anchor. I prayed for myself, for the other members of the survivors group, and for the social workers.

When the sessions finally ended for the survivors group, the social workers made sure we each had at least three phone numbers of trusting and caring people we could count on for continued support. I gave a small crystal angel to everybody, symbolic of our guardian angels protecting us on our continued paths.

In the end, I came away from the group experience understanding that I hadn't made my father do anything. He was the abuser; I was the child. Mostly, through the experience of working with these other women in the group, I came to understand something significant and surprising: There was nothing inherently bad about me. I did not, as I had assumed most of my life, have some hideous flaw. None of us did.

CHAPTER 21

LIVING THE QUESTIONS

I had completed my goal of participating in an incest survivors group, the place where I assumed I'd find the key that would unlock the answer to my pain. After a long, arduous, anxious climb, I had reached the top of the mountain. But it was cold at the top, and, instead of an inspiring view, I was engulfed in a thick, disorienting fog. I hadn't found the key. I didn't know where I was and I couldn't see where to look anymore. In fact, only now did I begin to grasp the sadness I felt by the loss of my family. Only now was what Dr. Mac told me sinking in: my parents were emotionally dead to me. And not only them, but my aunts and uncles and cousins, as well. It was as if my whole family had been lost in a horrible earthquake or fire, except there was no acknowledgment, no funeral, no memorial service, no flowers, no condolences from friends, acquaintances, or colleagues. And yet I knew they were still alive. It was yet another way I felt bound in Saran Wrap, isolated from everybody else. Acquaintances would ask about my family and I'd search for ways to deflect and change the conversation. In my grief, I felt alone with my pain. And with the many Scriptures lessons I had learned on forgiveness, I was also filled with confusion. Wasn't I the one breaking up the family? Was it right to deny my daughter a relationship with her grandparents? Yet I knew I had to protect her from my father. And neither she nor I deserved my mother's hurtful, black-velvet-gloved abuse anymore.

Lillian's one-hundredth birthday was in the spring of 1987. My cousins Matthew and Luke had called earlier wanting to organize a family reunion. I told them I couldn't do it. I could not attend. I couldn't explain why, knowing they'd never believe me. Matthew had visited me in Boston a couple of years before while attending a conference. We'd had dinner, and, as I'd driven him back to his hotel, he told me my father was the most ideal Christian he had ever met. I'd nearly driven off the road. But it was more than just the fear of not being believed. I had come to fear my father. I feared his money and his brains and the connections I was sure that he'd made in the construction industry. He had an image to maintain. He knew people who could destroy me and Tom and Grace and make it look like an accident. I'd mentioned this to one of the social workers in the group and she said I was surely exaggerating. I thought, *What don't you understand about domestic violence?* And so I chose to retreat from the reunion and my family without explanation.

I wasn't the only one in a group in that time. Tom was, too. Tom had attended a one-day conference for spouses and partners of abuse survivors held by Ellen Bass, author of *I Never Told Anyone*. Ellen encouraged the attendees to form a group of their own, which they did. Tom had his own issues to deal with. I was by no means an easy person to live with. There had been the drinking. There had been the depression and the moodiness. I rarely had any interest in sex, even less so since I'd stopped drinking. Sex seemed revolting to me. But I tried. I knew sex was supposed to be a special bond in a marriage and

I felt guilty about my reluctance. When we did have sex, I always had to create a safe environment. I played ocean waves on a cassette player and darkened the room. And there had been the grossly unfair things I had said to Tom, sometimes in anger, sometimes just because he was a man. "If you ever do anything to Grace, I swear I'll kill you," I had threatened, despite knowing that Tom was a caring and reliable father. There were eight other members of Tom's group, all men, and it was good for Tom to have people to talk with who understood.

Once, I asked Tom why he loved me. How could he? He said he respected how hard I was working to resolve my problems. He said I had a good heart and that I was doing a good job caring for Grace. Besides all that, he said he liked my smile. I was touched. And reassured. Of course, I disagreed with him about Grace. I was sure I was not a good enough mother.

Meanwhile, I had joined another group, this one at a local Catholic church, the church of a friend I'd met at a Tupperware party. The group was especially for mothers of small children and it consisted of two hours of weekly uninterrupted adult conversation, something we all could use as a break from the constant needs and demands of our kids. But the group had a spiritual focus and we also discussed Scriptures that might be applicable to parenting. It became a close, caring little community and I started to feel at home with them. We helped each other outside of the group, too. We gave each other rides or babysat for each other. If someone was sick, we'd bring meals. These women became role models for me as mothers, something, of course, I did not have in my own life experience. They also became friends.

I enjoyed the mothers group, but, for the most part, I was still heavily depressed. I did the incest survivors group again in the fall, joined by the other members of the earlier group and a couple of new members. Winter followed. I threw myself into the Christmas season, but, afterwards, it was just a typical cold, dreary, Boston winter. I had hoped the survivor's group would give me all the answers I needed, the key to my healing. It had not. I had learned I was not hideously flawed, but I still found myself grieving. During a session with Joan, I told her I still didn't know how to get to where I wanted to go. I still didn't have the answers.

"Live the questions," Joan told me.

I sat quietly, puzzled by her advice.

"Live the questions into the answers," she continued.

I remained puzzled. "I don't understand."

Joan was quiet. Then, after a long silence, she pulled a book off her shelf by famed German poet Rainer Maria Rilke, *Letters to a Young Poet*. She opened it to a passage and handed it to me and I read.

Be patient toward all that is unsolved in your heart and try to love the questions themselves, like locked rooms and like books that are now written in a very foreign tongue. Do not now seek the answers, which cannot be given you because you would not be able to live them. And the point is, to live everything. Live the questions now. Perhaps you will then gradually, without noticing it, live along some distant day into the answer.

After the session, I began thinking more and more about the passage. I found it incredibly profound. I was stunned that Joan wasn't going to give me any answers. I hadn't realized until that moment that she had none to give. Joan wasn't going to tell me to just accept my circumstances, either. The key was to live everything. "Live the questions, Sarah," she would often remind me from that point on, especially at those times when I wanted a concrete answer to something that I would later come to understand was an unanswerable mystery. "Live the questions into the answers." This was a new perspective for me to ponder. In other sessions, Joan would quote Saint Paul from Corinthians: "For now, we see in a glass darkly."

One time she told me that grief was like a circular stairway. It's far from a linear progression and so it takes longer to climb than a straight stairway. But as you continue climbing, such is the nature of a circular stairway that, during your inevitable stumbles, it becomes more and more difficult to fall all the way to the bottom, to the depth of your pain. And, with time, you climb a little bit higher and learn a little bit more about yourself, all the while developing ways to better cope. Joan said that it reminded her of the African-American spiritual song "Jacob's Ladder." *Every round goes higher and higher.*

One day, in 1989, I was home alone with Grace, now seven years old, and I glanced out of the window to see, of all people, my father, getting out of his Cadillac and walking toward the house. I'd had no contact with him for years. I felt my chest tighten and my heart begin to pound. He held something in his hand, and, as he got closer, I realized it was Suzie, the doll that had offered me comfort as a child, the doll he'd torn the hair off of and thrown in the garbage. He was gripping the doll carelessly by the arm, with her dress and braids oddly dangling. He came around to our back porch and knocked on the door and I opened it a crack. He said he'd come across the doll and wanted to return it to me.

"Thanks," I said, taking Suzie. "I have to go now." Then I closed the door and locked it. My father walked back down the steps and got into his car and drove away. This was followed by a full-blown anxiety attack. I called Tom and told him I needed him at home, and he came right away.

I began wondering what my father's ulterior motive was in stopping by our house. The doll had been an excuse. My father had knocked on the door just to confirm my whereabouts. Now he knew for certain where I lived. I was convinced my father wanted to harm my family. I found an all-female law firm that specialized in domestic abuse and one of the partners wrote my father a letter telling him in no uncertain terms that he was never again to contact me, or any member of my family. She sent it by both regular mail and certified mail. The letter mentioned the sexual assaults and that I had spent many years trying to heal. Any effort to try to contact me would be considered "harassment, trespass, and a violation of [my] privacy." If nothing else, I calculated that the letter would at least provide a record in case some strange accident would befall Tom and Grace and me.

In 1990, my grandmother died of pneumonia in a nursing home at the age of ninety-six. It had come upon her quickly. I did not attend her funeral. I knew my mother and sister would be there, and I knew I could not deal with any of the family. I could not be sociable. I could not be my mother's sweet Southern daughter. A month or so after the funeral, over a long weekend, I went by myself to visit my grandmother's grave in Asheville to pay my respects. I left flowers.

During that trip, I stayed with Aunt Iris, who was now an active ninety-eight year old and still living in her bed-and-breakfast home, though no longer taking guests outside of family. As we were seated in her den, she surprised me with my grandmother's diamond ring and wedding band. I was stunned. I was certain that I would never get the ring. This is when I asked Aunt Iris about the void between my mother and me. Did she have any understanding about our painful relationship? I mentioned the story I had briefly heard that one year at Christmas, about my grandmother calling the police on my mother and father. Aunt Iris filled in the details. As it happened, my grandmother and grandfather had actually taken the train to Peoria. They appealed to my parents to find a way to make things work, even offering to take me back with them until my parents could settle into a better schedule, one more conducive to taking care of an infant. My parents refused. I imagine the scene must have been ugly. Seeing no choice, my grandparents made a personal visit to the Peoria police station. The police were reluctant to interfere in what they most likely viewed as a private family matter, and, in the end, my grandparents could not bring themselves to press charges against their only daughter.

They returned to Asheville. There was a long silence after Aunt Iris told me these things and then I thanked her for telling me. I felt that I had now found a major puzzle piece. At the age of forty-three, another family secret had been revealed to me.

Two years later, at the age of one hundred, my Aunt Iris would pass away in her home, in her sleep. Tom and I attended her funeral while Grace, now ten, was away at Girl Scout Camp. We stayed in a hotel while my mother and her cousins stayed at Aunt Iris's house. At the funeral, Tom and I sat apart from the family. One of Iris's sisters-in-law approached us, annoyed, and admonished us not to make a scene by separating ourselves from everybody else. I felt as if it would make a scene either way. My mother and I didn't speak to each other the whole time, and, as I watched other family member interact with her, while leaving me alone, I couldn't help but wonder if they were all thinking, *what's the matter with Sarah?* I would reflect on this afterwards, on how deep an impact one's relationship with one's mother has on familial connections and sense of belonging. My relationship with my mother put me squarely on the outside of the family looking in. I no longer had any allies. I did not belong.

Back home, through the mothers group, I became more involved with the Catholic Church. Tom was Catholic, after all. We joined the church, but doing so required me to show my baptismal certificate. I traveled to Connecticut to our old Methodist church to retrieve a copy of it. I asked to go into the sanctuary and I sat in the pew where we all sat as a family and I thought of myself sitting there as a child and began to cry. The realization came to me then that God could never have made my parents love me. Choosing to be caring and loving are individual choices. Not even God's love can replace a childhood. But I also knew that I'd become aware of a force that had sustained me through all of the consuming darkness and confusion of my life.

I picked up my baptismal certificate from a woman who knew my family and she asked how we were doing. "I really don't know," I said.

"I don't keep in touch. That's the problem with dysfunctional families."
She nodded blankly and I said thanks and left.

Afterwards, I went to Hubbard Park, where, as a child, I had played on
the jungle gym and swing set and swum in the public pool with my sister
on hot summer days, much like this one. Now I was there to pray and
meditate. I drove my car up a narrow road, ascending nearly a thousand
feet to Castle Craig, a stone observation tower. I got out of the car and
hiked a short distance to an outcrop near the tower and sat down to admire
the surrounding hills overlooking the beautiful Quinnipiac River valley.

Then, thinking about the loss of my family and the loss of my childhood, I began to cry. And I wondered how I could ever get through
it, or be the mother I wanted to be for Grace, or be the wife I wanted
to be for Tom. As I sat there, my prayer book fell open to Psalm 27.

The LORD is my light and my salvation;
whom then shall I fear?
The LORD is the strength of my life;
of whom then shall I be afraid?

…For in the day of trouble he shall keep me safe
In his shelter;
He shall hide me in the secrecy of his dwelling
and set me high upon a rock.

… Though my father and my mother forsake me,
the LORD will sustain me.

…What if I had not believed that I should see the
goodness of the Lord in the land of the living?

…O tarry and await the Lord's pleasure;
Be strong, and he shall comfort your heart;
wait patiently for the Lord.

I started crying again. And from that rock, I decided to wait on the Lord, trusting that I would be sustained. And I would live the questions.

CHAPTER 22

THAT YOU MAY HAVE LIFE

When Lillian passed away not long after her 100th birthday in 1987, I did not attend her funeral, just as I would not attend my grandmother's three years later. My father would be there, of course, along with all my aunts, uncles, and cousins.

Shortly after Lillian died, I decided I needed to visit my cousin Luke, who was living close to my father in Connecticut. Luke and his wife had an eight-year-old daughter and an eleven-year-old son. I needed to warn him. Tom drove and was with me for support when I explained to Luke why he needed to make sure to never leave his children for any reason at all with my father. My confession came as a shock to Luke and his wife. They told me that the story my father had passed around was that our falling out had been over religious differences. But they believed me and thanked me.

All this time, my friend Pam was spending time in and out of mental institutions, still struggling with drug and mental health issues. Often, her son Jeffrey would stay with us during the course of her short hospitalizations. Eventually, Jeffrey was placed in foster care for about a year. Pam would ultimately get herself together and move with Jeffrey to Ohio, where she had family, but our friendship would never really be the same. Pam knew on some level that, during her worst days, she could not take care of her son, and yet she resented me for caring for him. But she also blamed herself. There was always a kind of underlying anger, and the intensity of emotions on her part made it awkward and difficult for us to keep in touch.

One day I received a letter from my Uncle Gene, my father's brother. He wanted me to know he'd been diagnosed with prostate cancer. In the letter was a picture of Brenda and me when I was three and she was six months. This was a treasure; I had no pictures at all of the two of us as children. He wrote that he wanted my mother's address, but I realized I didn't have it. I called Brenda for it, but she wouldn't give it to me, even after I explained it wasn't for me but for our uncle. Brenda was being protective; she'd obviously taken my mother's side.

This made me think of a time back when we were still taking trips to the shore. Brenda and I had talked about our father's abuse, remembering his anger and the silent dinners. I asked her if he'd ever attempted to sexually come on to her. "Once," she said, "but he stopped when I said I'd tell Mom." Then she changed the subject. By this time, Joan had described to me Brenda's identification with our mother. She was Brenda's role model. I could see this in Brenda's choice of husband—Bruce, a man quick to anger who often spoke to Brenda in harsh, denigrating terms in front of all of us. At the time, I took my pre-teen daughter aside, telling her to pay attention to the way Bruce talked to Brenda compared to how Tom talked to me.

I kept seeing Joan and we kept recommending books to each other. She introduced me to *Interior Castle* by the fourteenth-century Christian mystic St. Theresa of Avila. I read Julian of Norwich, too, and Hildegard of Bingen, St. Thérèse of Lisieux, and other mystics. I was also continuing my journaling, attending a journaling workshop every year. I would come back and share my journals with Joan. I was especially helped by the dialoguing exercises. At one point, I dialogued with my abuse, personalizing it for the purposes of engaging with it in a respectful "I-thou" manner. *You disgust me,* I wrote. *I wish I could kill you, but I can't without killing myself.* Sexual abuse replied: *I have taught you many things. Darkness can lead to light. Even Christ had to suffer hideously, and he died, but his light was not snuffed out.* Then I wrote: *How ironic, the thing that I hate and despise the most has been the impetus for so much learning in my life.* It was amazing to me, as I wrote these words, how transformative my spirituality was becoming, how my mind-set was tangibly changing from victim to survivor and beyond.

I dialogued with the Blessed Mother over the years, too, often lamenting the lack of a mother in my own life. By that time, Sister Theresa, the person who had started the mothers group had been transferred to another church. Ruth, who had been so much help with Pam and who had become like a surrogate mother to me in the process, had moved to Colorado. The leader of the prayer group had also moved away and the group had more or less fallen part. All of these influences represented a vital feminine aspect to my life that was now missing. In my journal, I wrote that it felt like Antarctica. It felt cold and dark and lonely. Even though Joan explained these instances as loss, I took them to be abandonment. Dialoguing with the Blessed Mother helped reconnect me with the motherly, feminine energy I'd missed.

I wrote about my need for a mother and how I wanted so much to be a good mother for Grace, yet I was essentially a motherless child myself. Worse, even, for my mother was still alive. *It has been my joy to watch you grow,* In the dialogue, Mary replied, *Your family told you you were unlovable, deserving of abuse. That scarring is incredibly deep. The miracle is that you can believe that you are lovable.* At that moment,

I imagined myself as an infant in my lonely crib. She picked me up and held me close and said, *I offer you my breast because you need to drink deeply of the milk of love, to know that there is plenty, to know that it is always there, to know the joy of it, the joy it brings me to nourish you, my child, my life.*

After that, I would go to sleep at nights seeing myself with my head on the Blessed Mother's lap, with her singing me a lullaby. My nightmares stopped. This experience of the Blessed Mother became as important to me as my vision experience. It was filled with feminine energy and notions of motherhood that had been absent from my childhood. I had no loving earthly mother. I thought of the women in my life—Aunt Iris and Brig, and even Joan—who had unconsciously become surrogates for me. The physical abandonment of me by my own mother when I was still in the crib would become a symbol of the emotional abandonment I would suffer from then on. She left me, and, worse, she left me to the whims of my father. All of this was now becoming clear to me. I wondered how I had survived it. Amazingly and ironically, I was becoming much stronger, knowing that I had. I tried to be open to where the processes of journaling, therapy, spiritual discipline, and connecting with friends were taking me.

In 1995, I received a letter from Martha, my father's older sister. She wrote that my father had moved to Florida and had been hospitalized three times in the past year. Like my Uncle Gene, my father, too, had been diagnosed with prostate cancer. "In case you care," she added. He was scheduled to have radium implants. "Don't you think it would be nice to send him a card?" she wrote. "Your dad and I aren't perfect. We have made many mistakes in the past, but life is short and it seems as if perhaps you would let bygones be bygones." Aunt Martha didn't know about the abuse. She had latched onto the "religious differences" story. I wrote her back telling her that my father's "abuse of me in my childhood is something I struggle with every day." I chose not to use the word "sexual." I was still afraid of my father and I didn't want it getting back to him. But I told Martha that bygones could not be bygones. There could be no forgiveness without acknowledgment and responsibility.

And then I wrote a letter to my father. I told him of the consequences of his actions. "I suffer from major anxiety and depression directly connected to your sexually abusing me as a child," I wrote. "I've been in therapy for the better part of twenty-three years. I am on antidepressant medication. I cannot describe to you the suffering, isolation, shame, and silence in my life, and the ongoing struggle I experience just to survive."

And yet, I opened a door for forgiveness. I continued: "In order for me to have any kind of relationship with you, a sincere, heartfelt written apology is necessary. Along with this apology, a reimbursement for twenty-three years of therapy and medication are necessary. I compute this figure to be $74,000." Even with his millions, I knew this was a reach. But, if the improbable happened, I planned on letting him write checks to sexual abuse and survivor charities. "Your apology and reimbursement will be a meaningful sign that you have changed and some recognition of my pain and suffering. In order for me to forgive you, I need to know that you assume responsibility for your hurtful actions toward me, that you are sorry for these actions and the pain and suffering they have caused me. These efforts at reconciliation will be a freely given gift, not only to me, but to yourself. I have been working on forgiving you. This letter is part of my forgiveness work." I closed the letter, saying I had compassion for anyone who suffers and was therefore sorry to hear of his illness.

I never heard from my father again.

Later, I would see the stage production of *The Phantom of the Opera* and take note of the incestuous overtones. The character of the Phantom was pathetic to me, and, for the first time, I began connecting the same feeling of contemptuous pity to my father, as opposed to the feelings I had had for years of someone who was powerful and threatening. As for my mother, Joan helped me eventually see that she had loved me as much as she could. I was clothed, fed, and properly schooled. But, for whatever reason, perhaps a history of her own abuse, my mother simply could not make herself available emotionally.

During all these years, starting after the group therapy, where I'd learned I was not hideously flawed; continuing with the mothers group, where I discovered motherly and family role models, along with friendships; to my continued sessions with Joan, who was providing me therapy with a strong spiritual component; to my coming to grips with the revelation about my mother leaving me unattended as an infant; to my slow but steady acceptance of the loss of my family; to my further involvement in the Catholic Church, my continued journaling—it was all a process of discovery and, in a sense, renewal. I was living the questions and, little by little, I was growing in faith and strength. I spent more time in prayer and meditation and spiritual reading. I began to feel more confident, more alive. As early as 1990, I had written in my journal that I was like a butterfly shedding her cocoon. And, in the years that followed, I felt a larger sense of well-being come over me. I had wonderful dreams at night. I even felt better physically, my neck and back problems receding.

By then I had read much of Joseph Campbell, the famous professor and author who'd extensively studied comparative religion and mythology. Campbell had written *The Hero with a Thousand Faces* and *The Power of Myth*, the latter of which was made into a documentary series with Bill Moyers. Campbell noted the spiritual symbolism of both the rose and the lotus, eastern and western religious symbols, respectively, the former complete with thorns and the latter complete with mud. There was a lesson in the juxtapositions and the need for both attributes of each symbol. It was the power of paradox. Once, in meditation, I saw the fishhooks that were embedded in the red heart that was with my mask become transformed into rose thorns. And then I saw a rose-bud blossoming into a Peace rose. "Honoring the rose within" became a new mantra for me. My journey was being transformed.

I felt myself wanting to take better care of myself. I had learned in the mothers group that one of the best ways to be there for your children is to take care of yourself first. I hadn't seen a doctor or dentist in years, what with my fear of being placed in such a vulnerable position. Now, I was ready to make appointments. With Joan's help, I wrote introductory letters first, letting the doctors know of my sexual abuse, history of anxiety and depression, my need to feel safe, and the importance of having all procedures carefully explained to me. Tom would arrange his schedule to be with me. Even so, I would need to prepare myself. Going to appointments, I'd pack a bag with a stuffed animal and headphones for listening to music. I'd take my anti-anxiety medication, too, and practice a technique where you relax your hands, thereby making it difficult if not impossible to tense up elsewhere in your body. To this day, I approach all of my medical appointments this way.

One day, I wrote a letter to Dr. Mac, apologizing for having walked out of his office on my last visit to see him and thanking him for all the help he had given me. He wrote a nice letter back and I felt as if I gained some closure on my time with him.

At one point, I even found myself dispensing wisdom. Grace's third-grade teacher had alerted me to some concerns she had with Grace's progress and I told her I just wanted my daughter to be happy and content. Later, I felt the need to clarify my remarks and I wrote the teacher a letter telling her that what I really wanted was a balance for Grace. "If contentment is the goal, then growth is stunted," I wrote. "Happiness is only one aspect of emotions," I said, writing that pain and suffering and loss are part of a full life, too. It was a perspective I could not have possibly seen just a few years before. I was beginning to integrate all of my emotions, accepting all of what I'd experienced as an expression of what it meant to be alive.

There were some significant changes in those years. Tom's mother passed away. I had bonded with her. Indeed I had bonded with the whole family. They had become my family. But I also bonded with Tom's mother in another, unlikely way. One time, I confided in her my history of sexual abuse at the hands of my father. She listened and then quietly replied, "My father sexually abused my younger sister. I walked in on them one day. I told my father if he ever did it again, I would kill him." It was more confirmation in my mind of something that, by then, I had definitively concluded: far from being a rare occurrence, family sexual abuse is a rampant phenomenon.

Tom's mother's funeral was well attended by family members near and far. Grace, seeing the size of the gathering, and no doubt thinking about how much time we had spent with Tom's family on holidays and visits and Sunday dinners, began to ask questions about her "other" grandparents. The last time I'd allowed her anywhere near my father had been the Christmas when she was one. She had no recollection of them and knew nothing about them. I told her that, as a child, I had been abused. "Abuse," I told her, "is when you've been hurt by someone so many times, you can't be with them anymore." I gave no further details at the time, although, later, when Grace would be in her later teens, I would tell her more. But, for the time being, my explanation seemed to satisfy Grace's curiosity.

Around this time, I left my job at the hospital and took a position at another hospital closer to where I lived. But I remained grounded. The mothers group was as valuable as anything. While the mothers met, the children were watched by retired and semi-retired women of the parish whom we referred to as the grandmothers, and so there were several levels of bonding. It became a wonderful experience of three generations interacting with each other at a level I had never encountered. These people became a family to me. We started doing yearly retreats, and, at the first one, Sister Theresa, who had founded the group, talked of the love God has for us from the very beginning, referencing Hosea 11 verse 1: *When Israel was a child, God loved him.* "It's a personal and enduring love," she said, adding, "And so when Sarah here was a child, God loved her." This was like a lightning bolt to me, to imagine that, during those unbearable years of abuse, God had loved me. God had loved me all along.

I continued my reading of the mystics during this time, too, and I continued with the imagery of the Blessed Mother, nourishing me with love and wisdom. I felt the Christ within me. I felt the love that, in turn, provided me with the ability to love Tom and Grace and others. I continued reading the Scriptures, finding particular relevance in Isaiah 55:

All who are thirsty come to the water. You who have no money, come and receive grain and eat. Come without paying, without cost. Drink wine and milk. Why spend your money for what is not bread? Your wages for what fails to satisfy? Heed me and you shall eat well, you shall delight in rich fare. Come to me, heedfully listen, that you may have life.

CHAPTER 23

HOME

In September 1996, Joan made an announcement to me. She was going to stop taking on new clients and, within the next year, finish with her existing ones. The following year, she'd be turning sixty-five and she was going to retire. I had started seeing her when she was fifty-three. Her final year would be the twelfth of our therapy. I would be turning fifty that year.

True to form, I was initially angry with her, walking out of her office. Later we talked as we walked to Boston Garden. Again, Joan reminded me of the difference between abandonment and loss. Then she pointed out the growth I had made in those twelve years, suggesting I focus on the strength, awareness, and social resources that I had developed. Of course she was right. And, in thinking the matter over, it occurred to me that I needed to do something extraordinary to mark that progress. I decided I needed to perform a ceremony in observance of the fact that I had, finally, after all these years, found my way. Back to my true self. Back to where I was always meant to be. Back home, in a sense. I called it "A Celebration of Being Home," and I invited three people: Joan, Sister Theresa, and a friend from the mothers group named Susan. I invited Tom, too, but he declined, feeling that it might be better with just these women.

We held it at Adelynrood, a retreat house I had visited annually. We gathered on May 31, 1997. I chose this day because it was the Catholic Feast of Visitation, commemorating Mary's visit with Elizabeth, who, after being barren in her old age, became pregnant with John the Baptist. Mary, of course, was pregnant at the time with Jesus. The story had always moved me. We held the ceremony outside on a sunny spring day. The azaleas were in bloom, along with a wonderful wisteria arbor and the grass was green after the long winter and the spring-green leaves of the trees had recently emerged. We sat on benches under a large shade tree on a grassy lawn next to a small meditative garden near the chapel. I brought a photographer to provide me with a record of the event.

I covered a small table with the Budweiser towel I always wrapped my mask in. On top, I placed the mask and the fishhook heart, along with a small icon of Mary holding her baby Jesus, and a small Bible my grandmother gave me. Surrounding the mask and heart were a dozen and a half candles held in crystal cupholders, each named for Jesus, the Blessed Mother, various saints, Dr. Mac, my guests that day, and others who had been of help to me over the years.

As Joan, Susan, and Sister Theresa arrived, I met them covered in a floor-length black caftan. I welcomed them and gave each a corsage, and, when they were seated on the benches under the tree, I played "When You Wish upon a Star" on my cassette player, the song I used to sing to myself as a child, gazing out of my window at night, looking up at the stars.

I opened with a prayer of gratitude and thanksgiving. Then we read the Servant's Song in Isaiah: "Here is my servant, whom I uphold...A bruised reed he shall not break, a dimly burning wick he shall not quench..." and "I am the Lord; I called you in my righteousness to open the eyes of the blind, to bring out prisoners from the dungeon and from the prisons those who sit in darkness." Joan read from Matthew: "Not a single sparrow falls to the ground outside your Father's care." Sister Theresa read the verse from Hosea that she'd acquainted me with, the verse that meant so much to me: "When Israel was a child, God loved him."

Then I brought out the dresses, the ones my father had boxed up and sent to me some ten years prior—the Easter dresses my mother had made and the orange dress she had made for my dance recital. We all walked under the wisteria arbor, and, on a paved area, I put the dresses into a metal trash can, just like the trash can my father had tossed my doll's hair into. I gave candles to Joan, Sister Theresa, and Susan, and we all lit them and dropped them into the can. For safety, I held a hose at the ready while we watched the fire. It was remarkably cleansing to watch the dresses burn, to see the transformation into black ash. The dresses were no more. At that point, with the help of my friends, I took off the black caftan. Underneath I had on a pretty, full-length dress, light blue, with white daisies. Back under the shade tree, Sister Theresa put a flowered hat on me while Susan adorned me with a corsage. Joan slipped a necklace around my neck that was of a mother and child in a heart shape.

That was followed by the song, "Moon River." I read some poetry and then we played "Someday My Prince Will Come," from *Cinderella*. Together, we read Psalm 27, "The LORD is my light and my salvation."

I asked everyone to pick flowers to put around the mask and cover the fishhooks in the heart. I cut off the Saran Wrap and bathed the face of the mask. I was wearing my grandmother's ring that I had worn since Aunt Iris had given it to me and I slid it off and replaced it with a blue sapphire ring. There was too much pain around my grandmother's ring and I decided I didn't want to wear it anymore. Taking it off was just one more transformative symbol.

After that, Joan and I read the children's book, *Knots on a Counting Rope*, a poetic tale about a young Native American boy being told a story by his wise grandfather. The counting rope symbolizes each time the boy hears the story, and thus recounts the gradual growth and strengthening of his self-reliance, despite obstacles, including his own blindness. We changed the boy to a girl and the grandfather to a grandmother. I read the parts of the girl while Joan read the parts of the grandmother. The story had always touched and moved me and it seemed especially appropriate for the ceremony, especially with Joan reading the parts of the wise mentor.

I had gift bags for everyone that included Gunilla Norris's book *Being Home*. In return, Joan gave me a two-volume collection of the breviary with inclusive language, and a copy of *The Little Prince*. Susan gave me an angel and Sister Theresa gave me a beautiful card. Finally, I arranged for a dinner at the retreat center and we ate together.

The ceremony marked a milestone, not just the completion of my counseling with Joan, but a turning of the page. I'd become a different person. I had grown in those years, emotionally and spiritually. It had become time to say goodbye, in a sense, to the person I had been. And yet, I knew she would always be with me. The little girl, especially, I could never leave. But now I could extricate myself from the wreckage. I could stand beside it. I could view it more objectively. I would probably never be able to consider my childhood dispassionately, but I could now at least feel the emotions without crumbling. The abuse no longer controlled me as much. I learned to respond more and react less.

More than anything, Joan helped me see that I was not deserving of the shame I'd felt for all those years. The shame was not who I was. "It's a lie," she'd told me. "It is not your truth." She had helped me discover who I really was. I was worthy of better. I was worthy of a life that tended toward completion of love and happiness. I could have dreams. It was okay to ask for things. And I was worthy of love. I was not a perfect mother or wife, but I was certainly good enough. I had found and grown the core that Joan had depicted in the seesaw diagram that had asked, "Who is Sarah?" I could move forward. I could live. Really live. And I could do so secure in the knowledge that I had the wherewithal now to not only survive but to flourish. I was protected now from the past. I was safe now. I was home.

CHAPTER 24

CHANGES

I had two more sessions with Joan. The first was to process my feelings about the ceremony. There was much to celebrate in terms of all the ways I had grown and changed, including my ability to share my story with trusting and caring friends. But it was bittersweet, knowing my time with her was coming to a close. For twelve years, Joan had been my therapist, my mentor, and my spiritual guide. It was hard to imagine my life without her. She suggested that perhaps I should find another therapist, but of course I had no interest in trying to replace her. Our very last visit was more or less to say goodbye. She gave me an audio copy of *Knots on a Counting Rope* that she had recorded herself on cassette. I'd asked her to do so, so that I could hear her voice again. I gave her an angel. Joan had been an angel to me.

That summer at my annual journaling workshop, I dialogued with Joan. The exercise made me break down and I left the room, journaling in my car out in the parking lot so that my uncontrolled sobs wouldn't interrupt the others. At the annual mothers group retreat, I shared how much I missed Joan and one of my friends there said, "Sarah, it must be like losing your mother." I was touched that the enormity of my loss was appreciated.

During all this time, my profession had been drastically changing. In the 1990s, health maintenance organizations were shifting the focus of medicine and health care to metrics and cost savings. In maternity wards, new mothers were sent home after only twenty-four hours, forty-eight after a cesarean section. Eventually, after numerous documented readmissions for severe complications, Congress passed the Newborns and Mothers' Health Protection Act (NMHPA) in 1996, mandating forty-eight-hour stays for standard deliveries and up to ninety-six-hour stays for C-sections.

Before the passage of the NMHPA, I found myself feeling anxious about the direction health care was headed. Decisions were now essentially being made about a person's health care at the HMO level. And yet it was people like me, health-care workers, who were bearing the liability, should something go wrong. More importantly, I could not tolerate the limited care women were getting. I decided I needed to do something else. Even with the passage of the NMHPA, I could see the writing on the wall. Health care was no longer functioning the way it did before.

I thought about how much I had enjoyed the teaching aspects of my work, especially the teaching of mother-baby care and helping new mothers and their babies learn the skill of breast feeding. I decided to change directions and became a lactation consultant. Scientific research was pointing toward the health benefits of breast feeding, and, by the late 1980s, standards had been set for lactation consultants. I sat for an examination and became certified.

My work took me on home visits to new mothers. I liked what I was doing and I liked the independence, but driving around the towns north of Boston, without the benefit of GPS, was taxing, especially in the winter months. Winter itself was wearing on me, the cold, the ice, the snow, the dreariness. At one point, I broke an ankle slipping on black ice. Meanwhile, my next door neighbor and her partner would spend their winters in Florida every year. I'd see them coming back rested and suntanned. The idea appealed to me and I put it in the back of my mind. I even started setting some money aside, thinking maybe someday it could be Tom and me going to Florida for the winter.

At one point, a lactation program was opening up at a hospital at a women's center on the North Shore. I interviewed to head the program. It was going to have an inpatient and outpatient component and I was excited about it. I got the job but found out shortly thereafter that I'd been given the position instead of someone who had been there for years. This person was well liked by a certain faction of people who were determined to make things difficult for me. I found myself dragged into the politics of the organization and my excitement for the job waned quickly after that. It saddened me to leave, but I left, knowing it was the best thing for me.

For a short time after that, until I could figure out what to do, I went to work in a birding supply store. I'd been part of an Audubon birding group and had enjoyed visiting a reserve on Plum Island off of Boston's North Shore, where we would see all manner of birds. Grace was getting ready to go off to college and although I continued to struggle to give myself permission to do things for myself, I had managed to allow myself the pleasure of birding. I knew the bird store, having bought feeders and other supplies there, and asked the owner for a part-time job. I was too burned out, both physically and mentally, to consider full-time nursing. The owner of the bird store hired me for three days a week and I stayed on about six months, a nice hiatus from the stresses of my health-care work. In 1999, I found a position as a lactation consultant in a teaching hospital in Boston, again with an inpatient-outpatient component.

In the fall of 2000, Grace went off to college. My baby was now a young woman. I forced myself not to cry in front of her when we said our goodbyes at her dorm as we dropped her off. A huge chapter in my life had now closed.

Tom continued to work. One morning in September of 2001, he called me from his office. I was getting ready to take my morning walk. It was a beautiful day in New England, the sky a clear, cloudless blue. "Do you have the news on?" he said.

"Why?"

"A plane hit the World Trade Center."

Like everyone else, I initially imagined a small plane had errantly crashed into the building. Who could have conceived of a passenger airliner being used as a weapon of terror? I turned on the news and was shocked to see the amount of smoke emanating from the North Tower. And then I watched as the second plane hit the South Tower. Later, it would be determined that both planes had left from Boston that morning. I canceled a dentist appointment in the city for that day and my call to them was how they learned the news. This was before the time of instant updates on your laptop or smartphone. The dentist office closed, like most businesses did. Like the rest of America, I spent the balance of the day glued to the TV coverage. I did venture out to 11:30 Mass. The church was packed, everyone seeking solace and comfort.

For weeks, I felt a deep sadness about the events of that day. With the two flights originating in Boston, many on board had been residents of the greater Boston area, and, for a while, it seemed as if there was a funeral every day for somebody lost in the attacks, often several funerals a day. The idea of terrorism was suddenly very real. A couple of times after the attacks, I was riding the subway when power outages made it stop. That had happened before, from time to time, but, now when it did, things felt different. The subway car would become eerily quiet. What was going on? Was the city being besieged? Shortly, after a period of just a few minutes that always felt much longer, the train would start up again like normal.

Just before Thanksgiving, Tom and I were met with grief on a more personal level. His oldest sister, Lisa, passed away. Suffering from Turner Syndrome her whole life, she had beaten the odds by far, living to be sixty when she hadn't been expected to live beyond infancy. But, in her waning weeks, her personality had changed. Her optimism made way for cynicism. She'd become argumentative. We took her out for her birthday and invited her out to dinner to help celebrate Tom's birthday that year and found her very difficult to be with on both occasions. She'd been having work done on her house, the family house, and we put her behavior change down to stress from the remodeling.

For that year, Tom and I decided to make Thanksgiving a small affair, just us and Grace. This hurt Lisa's feelings deeply, and no amount of explaining seemed to help. After she argued with Tom on the phone to where he had to hang up, I called Lisa back and promised we'd get together after Thanksgiving and celebrate Christmas with her. That would be the last time Tom or I spoke to her. On the Monday morning of Thanksgiving week, the workers at her house found her dead. She had died in her sleep.

Our sadness was tinged with guilt. Tom had the responsibility of closing and selling the house, making things for him even more difficult. For my part, I tried to remember Lisa as the sweet, bright person she'd been, always cheerful in the face of her condition, strengthened by her faith. Her faith, in fact, had been everything to her. She was a devoted Catholic, always attending daily Mass, singing in the choir, and teaching CCD classes. Her pride and joy was a medal that had been blessed by Cardinal Bernard Law, Archbishop Emeritus of Boston.

In retrospect, the timing of her death was perhaps fortuitous. Lisa would not have survived the blow that was soon coming. In early 2002, the *Boston Globe* started running articles about certain transgressions within the Church, even involving Cardinal Law. And everything we thought we knew about the Catholic Church was about to be turned upside down.

CHAPTER 25

BETRAYED BY THE CHURCH

With 9/11 and with Lisa's death, the end of 2001 was especially stressful for me. My arthritis began flaring up. I felt pain in my back, knees, shoulders, everywhere. Somewhere in that time period, I began taking voice lessons with a choral group, the lessons I was denied as a child. Like the birding, this was another thing I decided to do for myself, something I gave myself permission to do. Surprisingly, I noticed a reduction of pain when I sang, highlighting the connection between the emotional and the physical. Singing became another therapy, of sorts. But I still had health issues, including stomach problems that were eventually linked to an intolerance of gluten. I had sinus problems, too. Ultimately, I went to a chiropractor to help manage my arthritis pain and it turned out she also specialized in diet. When, per her advice, I took gluten and other foods out of my diet, my sinuses cleared up and so did my stomach problems. My arthritis became manageable. But the change in diet meant that a lot of comfort foods I liked were now off limits. It was another painful loss.

Then came a blow I would never have expected. The *Boston Globe's* "Spotlight" team of investigative reporters started uncovering widespread child sexual abuse by Catholic priests in the Archdiocese of Boston. The abuse had been known and covered up by many within the Church, including Cardinal Law.

Reports had made the papers as early as the summer of 2001, but they always seemed like anomalies. A single priest here, a single priest there. There were hundreds and hundreds of priests in the diocese, after all. I knew that, within any institution, you can find bad seeds. But the *Globe* articles indicated a systemic problem. And the deeper the investigation went, the deeper the problem was revealed to be.

The tipping point came in 2002, with criminal charges brought against five Boston priests. One priest, John Geoghan, was accused of abuse involving 130 children. All five priests were convicted and sentenced to prison. That's when it came out that the abuses had been known by local bishops and Cardinal Law. During the trials, Cardinal Law was deposed and internal Church documents were forced to the surface. Among other revelations, it became known that Geoghan had simply been moved from one unsuspecting parish to the next, keeping him ahead of the rumors and accusations that had been following him. And yet, he remained a priest. Other priests had been sent on "sabbaticals" and then allowed to return to their duties. The victims and their families who had made their abuse known to Church authorities had, meanwhile, been paid to keep their silence and made to sign nondisclosure agreements, each of them told that "appropriate" measures were being taken to ensure that what happened to them would never again happen to anyone else, even as it was continuing to happen.

Newsweek did a story profiling Patrick McSorley, one of those 130 victims of Geoghan, a twenty-seven year old who had been abused at the age of twelve. Geoghan had discovered that Patrick's father had committed suicide a few years before and used the knowledge as a pretext to take the boy out for ice cream, an act Patrick's mother was naturally grateful for. On the way home, Geoghan fondled Patrick while fondling himself. The case was illustrative: the priests were not just pedophiles, but predators, looking for weaknesses, coldly calculating their moves to take advantage of the most vulnerable. In 2004, Patrick McSorley would be found dead of a drug overdose. Anthony Muzzi Jr., another victim, spoke of the love and respect people in the Church had for Geoghan, making it virtually impossible for a child to say anything at all about his actions. Anthony had been abused by Geoghan back in the 1960s, shockingly revealing the length of time Geoghan had been preying on children. In that time, he'd continued his priestly duties through the terms of five bishops and two cardinals.

Emboldened by the convictions and the coverage by the *Globe*, people started coming out by the hundreds to speak about the abuse they had suffered at the hands of other Catholic priests. Reports of abuse became nationwide. Then worldwide. In no time, the number of people reporting the abuse was in the thousands. In time, there would be over 11,000 allegations involving more than 4,000 priests in the United States alone. It was nothing less than an epidemic. And the accompanying cover-ups by the Church's bishops and cardinals represented to me nothing less than institutionalized evil.

Over the course of months and years, I watched this all play out, in the papers, on TV, on the internet. I fell into a depression. Stories came out of the shame the victims had felt, believing they were most likely headed to hell for the activities they had engaged in with these revered men of God. I knew of that shame, and, at times, I felt as if I was being abused all over again, long after I had thought I had put my abuse behind me, that I had found my way to healing. I wrote in my journal, "The crisis feels like a hideous nightmare that you cannot wake up from." In the first few months after the scandal broke, I felt sick. I read about the deals the Church had made with accusers and the intimidation they used to keep the abuse from becoming public. So much of my life had been tied up in the Church. The Church had helped me heal from the scars of the exact same kind of abuse it was now known to have inflicted. My father might have been a monster, but at least he never pretended to be a man of God. These were men who were regarded as living lives of prayer, holiness, and service. When a priest walked into a room, you stood in reverence. How could I ever consult with a priest again about a spiritual matter? These were men who were supposedly reflections of God's love, celebrating the sacred sacraments of the altar. How could I ever again confide in a priest or trust a priest? I felt betrayed, I felt lost. I was a boat that had lost its anchor, aimlessly adrift.

I didn't have Joan to talk to and so I asked Sister Anne, the sister who had taken over the leadership for Sister Theresa in the mothers group, if she knew of a spiritual retreat center I could attend. Adelynrood was a summer retreat house and closed for the winter. I didn't feel I needed a psychologist anymore. And besides, I needed to talk to someone in the Church, someone who was grappling with this same issue, someone who understood how I felt. Sister Anne recommended a spiritual center in Maine that was open year-round, the Marie Joseph Spiritual Center. I would go for long weekends every couple of months and talk to Sister Agnes, a spiritual counselor, grateful to be able to commiserate about a tragedy so close to all of our hearts. The Church was more than the priests, we agreed, but we were nonetheless shell-shocked. "I grieve with you," said the counselor.

A couple of months after the scandal broke, there was a sharing session at our parish, presided over by our pastor and a local bishop, where people could speak their minds. Two priests, no longer within our parish, had been found guilty of abuse that had occurred years before. One woman stood up and said, "I have been dutifully confessing my sins every week. And now I find that I confessed them to a pedophile? How can I ever again confess to a Catholic priest?" It was a question everyone had. People called for resignations and prison terms. In another session, a woman stood up and said her nephew had committed suicide in his twenties. Nobody knew why at the time, but they knew now that one of the guilty priests had accompanied him on camping trips when he was just a boy. It wasn't hard to make the connection.

During Lent, a life-size black cross went up in the church and a deacon asked the children of a second-grade CCD class to bring in photos of themselves, which were then glued to the cross. It was a powerful metaphor of the suffering of the sexually abused children, many of whom were now adults. These attempts at healing, at acknowledging the wrongdoings, were few and far between, and almost never by the upper echelons of the Church. At times, I wanted to distance myself completely from the Church. It was no longer the refuge it had been. It was hard going to Mass. I would look at the priest and wonder, *has this man committed abuse? Did he know of abuse, yet remain silent? Did he do the right thing and report the abuse, only to have his report ignored or, worse, covered up?* But groups like the mothers group made me realize that I couldn't leave. Since the mothers group, I'd also joined a mid-life women's group and Tom and I had joined a couples group. The Church had become my second family. More than anything, it's where I worshipped. And if I did leave the Church, was it right to do so without first trying to affect change? On the other hand, was it hypocritical to stay? How could I maintain my integrity in the face of the crimes that had been committed within the Church?

There were a lot of us asking these same questions. Early on, there was a meeting at a church in Wellesley, where hundreds attended to celebrate Mass, everyone collectively praying for direction and guidance. From that was born the Voice of the Faithful, an

organization committed to supporting survivors of abuse, supporting priests of integrity (many innocent priests were suffering from
the horrendous publicity of the scandal), and shaping structural
change within the Catholic Church. We picketed the Cathedral
of the Holy Cross, demanding the resignation of Cardinal Law. In
December 2002, Law would, in fact, resign. I support Voice of the
Faithful to this day. I also support Bishop-Accountability.org, an
organization committed to documenting abuse and maintaining a
database of abusers. One of their goals is to post on their website
every available document and report regarding the sexual abuse
crisis.

It became hard to look at the Church the same way. One of the
members of the mid-life women's club told us that, years before,
her brother had been abused by a priest in our parish and had
been subsequently paid off to keep quiet. Tom and I put less in
the collection plate. Every year, Cardinal Law had a special collection known as the Cardinal's Appeal. That year's theme was "The
Promise of Tomorrow." Tom and I didn't give. The only promise
I wanted was a promise that our clergy could be trusted with our
children. We donated less to the Church and more to organizations
like the Salvation Army and women's shelters. Meanwhile, Voice of
the Faithful struggled to get accepted by the Church. Our parish's
lay advisory committee voted that the parish should be a chapter
of the Voice of the Faithful. Our priest began to initiate the process
but was stopped by the bishop, who declared it "inappropriate."
In fact, the Church at the highest levels continued to defend itself
aggressively, playing victim, claiming that the media had overblown
the story.

For obvious reasons, I was also tortured by the patriarchy of the
Church. I had never felt comfortable calling a priest Father. The word
"father" was painful to me on a visceral level, although Tom was

certainly a good father, and I knew other good fathers. At best, I was conflicted by the term. I tried to think instead of the female energy of the Church, from the Blessed Mother on down. I thought of Saint Teresa and Julian of Norwich. I thought of Mother Teresa, and, in times when I felt overwhelmed, I thought of her contention that, "We cannot do great things, only small things with great love." And so I continued battling my depression, searching and coping as best I could, doing small things, and trying to figure out how to move on.

CHAPTER 26

MOURNING

As time went on, the sexual abuse nightmare continued to unfold. In April of 2002, the *Boston Globe* published a statement from the Vatican after a two-day meeting between cardinals of the United States, leadership of the US Catholic Conference of Bishops, and the heads of several offices of the Holy See. The statement addressed the issues of the sexual abuse, but parts of it were self-serving and parts of it were downright bizarre. The participants of the meeting "recognized the gravity" of the problem, the statement read, "even if the cases of true pedophilia on the part of priests…are few." The Church hierarchy maintained that "almost all the cases involved adolescents and therefore were not cases of true pedophilia."

It was more denial. And it got worse. "We…propose a special process for cases which are not notorious, but where the diocesan bishop considers the priest a threat for the protection of children and young people, in order to avoid grave scandal in the future and to safeguard the common good of the Church." And there it was, the real concern:

to avoid scandal for the common good of the Church. I wondered as I read the statement whether there was room for concern about the victims, or their families, more of whom seemed to be coming forward every day. We continued, as rank and file members of the Church, to continue to press for change and accountability.

By then, the Church had put together a program called Protecting God's Children, which was designed to promote awareness and provide training and guidelines for those within the Church who interacted with children, including those who came in as volunteers. But, at one point, another article in *Newsweek* quoted the Church bishops saying that the Church could never have a "zero" policy of child sexual abuse. Exceptions were reasonable if it was the priest's only offense, or if, perhaps, the priest had been under the influence of alcohol. I was stunned by the obvious disconnect between these official positions and reality. The insularity of those in positions of Catholic power was mind-blowing. I couldn't help but draw a parallel in my mind to the denial I had seen in my own family.

Then came the news of Patrick McSorley's drug overdose in February of 2004. Speaking out against Geoghan, he had been one of the main voices for the victims. It seemed as if he had put it all together and moved beyond the anger, the shame, and the grief. It had taken so much courage to come forward. He'd had to climb over so many obstacles. He'd been so resolute standing in front of the microphones and testifying in court against Geoghan. Patrick McSorley succumbing to the stresses made me wonder about my own ability to handle the emotions I'd been feeling.

One day it all became too much for me and I did something I hadn't done in fifteen years. I had a drink. I wanted a glass of wine to relax, to relieve the stress I was feeling from the scandal. Then I had another glass, but that was it. Just the two. The next day, I also had two. The day after that, I had three. Then four. Quickly, my drinking escalated. Grace was off at college and Tom, though he would come home for dinner, would frequently leave afterwards for meetings as town engineer, leaving me alone to drink in the evenings. I noticed my memory was starting to become affected. My spiritual disciplines were falling off, too.

About that time, I started thinking about taking my journals and turning them into a book, a memoir of my survival. Madeleine L'Engle, author of *A Wrinkle in Time*, had an annual writers workshop at Holy Cross Monastery in New York State on the Hudson that I had attended. I took a couple of other writing courses after that. To write my memoir with everything else that was going on, I knew I needed to maintain my balance. I needed to be sober.

Grace's academic path, meanwhile, had taken her to Scotland, to the University of Stirling. Tom and I went over for her graduation in 2004. Stirling was known as the gateway to the Scottish Highlands and it reminded me very much of the mountains of North Carolina. Indeed, many Scotch-Irish had settled in North Carolina and through-out Appalachia and I felt as though I was visiting my roots. After graduation, Grace started a sabbatical year in Northern Ireland before going to law school. Tom flew back to Boston, and I attended a week-long spiritual retreat on the tiny island of Iona in the Inner Hebrides off the western coast of Scotland.

Founded in 563 by Saint Columba, Iona Abbey is a monastery on the island. Its members were the first people to bring Christianity to Scotland. The monastery undertook the production of written man-uscripts and books of importance and there's some evidence that the *Book of Kells*, a vibrantly illustrated manuscript containing the four Gospels of the New Testament, was produced there. In 1203, the Benedictines established a new monastery there, replacing the original, humble wooden structure with a stone building. This was eventually dismantled and abandoned during the Scottish Reformation in the

1500s, but, during the Depression in the 1930s, Reverend George MacLeod of Glasgow enlisted the help of out-of-work skilled laborers, who came together to rebuild the abbey and form a religious community on the island, lay people right alongside ministers and priests. The ecumenical community included men and women of many different Christian faiths and developed its own daily and Sunday liturgy and prayers.

We arrived by ferry. The retreat was for six days and there were around a hundred of us, people from all over. The island was only three square miles, with maybe a hundred inhabitants. There were probably more sheep on the island than people. There were bed-and-breakfasts on the island and a single pub, which I managed to stay away from.

I was taken by the manner of certain prayers in the Abbey. Some started with "Eternal Friend," and I'd never heard God referred to in such a way. There was a blessing which went, "May God write a message in your heart. May you read it and understand it. May you live it in your life." There was a big, arched window in the Abbey above the altar from which you could see the water, and, one day, I saw a sailboat with red sails and thought of Jesus and his disciples on the Sea of Galilee. The sheep around the Abbey reminded me of the Psalm: "The Lord is my shepherd." At one point during my stay, I lit a candle in the Abbey for my mother and thought about broken relationships and loss and suffering.

One day, we took a ferry to the site of Fingal's Cave, a tall and large volcanic cave of incredible acoustics that the ocean crashes into. Felix Mendelssohn visited the cave in 1829 and wrote an overture inspired by the strange and beautiful echoes he heard there. There were about thirty of us on the visit and we sang the "Celtic Alleluia" and "Amazing Grace" in four part harmony and the sound was exquisite. Afterwards, we walked over the top of the cave, too, and saw puffins. These are small birds with brightly colored beaks that I had never seen before.

Usually they're out to sea, but this just happened to be the time of year when they were nesting. It was a very rare sight. Puffins have an appreciation for people, since their presence has a tendency to scare away seagulls, a predator of the puffins.

On another day, there was a pilgrimage, a three mile walk. Because of my arthritis, I followed along for a mile of it. We began at St. Martin's Cross, a Celtic cross outside of the Abbey that had been standing since the sixth century. At the center of the cross was the Madonna and child. We walked to the abandoned, partially destroyed nunnery that had been built not long after the monastery back in the 1200s. Augustinian nuns had lived there for three-hundred years. We reflected in silence about the important women in our lives. We heard a poem called "Because She Cares" by the Scottish poet Nancy Somerville: "Each day, God the mother walks with me. She holds my hand at busy crossroads and reminds me to be careful because it matters to her what happens to me." Then we went to the only crossroads on the island, where people met and exchanged news and goods. We heard a meditation there about crossroads, of accepting joys and sorrows, and the importance of the choices we make. I felt as if my life was at a crossroads and the meditation spoke to me. I made a decision then and there to commit to sobriety and I prayed for God's help and guidance.

The night before our group left was a Thursday, just like the night of the Last Supper. We held Communion in the abbey and there were tables set up around the altar. One older man with Parkinson's and halting speech spoke, from his wheelchair, the words that Jesus had spoken during the Last Supper and I was never so moved by Communion. We gave Communion to each other, which was deeply felt by everyone. We were just regular people, and the lack of formality strangely made it feel more powerful.

The next day we had a parting blessing and we all said our goodbyes. I'd made a friend named Kathy and before I got on the ferry that would take me back to the mainland, she said, "Sarah, I don't know if you're aware of recovery culture, but feeling is good and numbness is a lie. We can only feel joy if we feel sorrow." As we hugged each other with tears in our eyes, I knew she was right.

I came back to the States refreshed, feeling better about life, more motivated to write the book, and determined to maintain my sobriety. In my journal workshop later that summer, I journaled with drinking and became aware that I had either been drinking or taking prescribed psychiatric medication since the age of nineteen, with the drinking frequently taking the place of the antidepressants. In denial, I'd stop taking the pills, soon become depressed, then turn to alcohol. Drinking had proven a poor and destructive substitute. I called my primary care physician and had her prescribe the antidepressants again, promising myself to not go off them.

I began my spiritual disciplines again, and, about this time, my spirituality took a significant turn. I thought of other religions. Catholicism, indeed, Christianity, did not, it seemed to me, hold a monopoly on universal truth. The Catholic Church reminded me of my treasured doll Suzie. After my father had mutilated her, she was different and I could never see her the same way again. Boston was diverse in religions and I had been exposed to many other faiths through friends and coworkers who were Jewish or Hindu or Muslim or Buddhist. And I had read much about other religions. Each seemed to represent a unique path, but all were concerned with the universal questions of truth, wisdom, love, compassion, suffering, and death. One day, I came across a quote from His Holiness the Dalai Lama, whose book *The Art of Happiness* I had read. When asked what his religion was, he said, "My religion is kindness." I decided to make that my religion, too. I could not divorce myself from the Catholic Church and my friends who were a part of it. I saw myself as a recovering Catholic, trying to live the teachings of Jesus. And I adopted a new religion. My religion would be kindness.

In early November of that year, I got a call from my cousin Luke. My father was losing his battle with cancer. In fact, he was in hospice with only a few weeks to live. I called his wife Cynthia, getting the phone number from Luke. I, of course, did not have it. This was in the days of the landline and I was able to have Tom listen in on an extension for moral support as I told Cynthia I was sorry that her husband was so ill. I told her I was interested in reconciliation. I had forgiven my father, who now seemed not dangerous but pathetic to me, and, if there was a way to let him know, before his death, that I had forgiven him, it seemed like I should. But the reconciliation, if there were to be one, would have to be on my terms. I needed an apology from my father. I needed contrition. Thinking of the letter I had written to him in 1995, that contrition needed to take the form of two checks totaling $74,000, one to Rosie's Place, a Boston charity for homeless women, and one to Incest Resources, part of the Cambridge Women's Center.

I asked Cynthia if she had read that letter. She had not. She said that my father had told her of the sexual abuse. He felt "terrible" about it and my divorcing myself from the family had been extremely difficult for him. His call to me years before saying he'd wanted "a loving family" was, according to Cynthia, a request for forgiveness that I had, in their minds, withheld through my silence and withdrawal. She also said she could not understand how my father could have done the things he had supposedly done because he was "such a wonderful man." I sensed her sympathy for my father and even some denial and it reminded me of the priests once again, the charming priests whom nobody would believe could have done such monstrous things. Except, of course, they had.

I asked Cynthia if she would approach my father with my request. "Probably not," she said.

"Would you at least let him know I called to offer reconciliation?" I said.

217

"I'll think about it," she said.

I told her once more that I was sorry she was losing her husband and we ended the conversation. Then I fell into Tom's arms. "You did good," he told me.

I called Brenda, too. She hadn't heard that our father was in hospice. She, too, had divorced herself from him. But she was still in touch with our mother and still feeling anger at me for separating from her. I couldn't help but notice the harsh, critical tone of my mother in my sister's voice.

Cynthia called me on December 21. My father had passed away early that morning, she said. I thanked her for the call, knowing she hadn't talked to him about the subject of our earlier phone call. Then I called Brenda to pass along the news. She said she appreciated the call, but the conversation, like all of our conversations, was stilted and awkward.

After hanging up, I thought of my father and felt a sadness wash over me, a sadness that I was never able to experience a caring father–daughter relationship. A sadness that I had never had a father who saw me, heard me, or respected me as his daughter. And I felt a sadness that, in the end, there was nothing about his death for me to mourn.

CHAPTER 27

ONE MORE MIRACLE

I did not attend my father's funeral; it didn't make sense to me to attend. I had nothing to grieve. Plus I hadn't interacted with anybody on that side of the family for nearly two decades. My presence might have been a distraction and I didn't want to intrude. I didn't share the news with anybody, either. Besides Tom and Grace, nobody around me knew, not friends, not coworkers, not even members of Tom's family. I didn't feel up to receiving condolences that would have meant nothing to me. I couldn't fake feelings of grief and I didn't want to have to explain why I didn't have any. Too, I was afraid someone would ask about the funeral. How would I justify not going? You're supposed to honor your mother and father.

Secretly, I felt overwhelming relief. I felt freedom. My lifelong anxiety about having my father further harass or hurt me and my family died with him. It felt like a rebirth of sorts. Nevertheless, I was still struggling with the Catholic Church abuse scandal, and, making things worse, another long winter was setting in. After the holiday season, I found myself depressed and anxious. My arthritis was flaring up. That winter, I slipped on the ice and hurt my knee. Coupled with the arthritis, I had to go on medical disability. Through it all, focusing on my disciplines, going to the spiritual center in Maine, and staying connected with my friends, I managed to hang onto my sobriety. To focus on my health, I had to stop working on my book and I let go of my committee work with the Voice of the Faithful.

After weeks of physical therapy, anti-inflammatories, and pain management, I was able to get back to work, but only for half-days. Ultimately, I knew I had to let go of my part-time benefited position. Until the medical leave, I'd been working eight- to ten-hour days, plus the commute. I knew I couldn't do it anymore, especially in the winter and especially with the arthritis. I went to a per diem position, working only one or two days a week as needed, part-time, but far from certain. Yet another loss. Work had given me purpose, routine, and a reliable income. It had always been important for me to contribute to the household. My reliable part-time work had been an anchor.

Then came news of Cardinal Law. He'd resigned as Cardinal Archbishop of Boston but had been reassigned to the Vatican. Now he was made archpriest of St. Mary Major Basilica in Rome, an important cathedral with a history that went back to 432 AD. The move once again highlighted the tone-deafness of the Church and fed my feelings of betrayal and despair. Once again, it felt as though I was reliving the pain of my childhood.

I continued my journaling and tried to remember what I'd learned: that I was responsible for my own happiness, which meant giving myself what I needed. I continued with my singing lessons, and, as the spring came around, I did some birding and took long walks with members of the mothers group. As the summer came along, I began to feel hopeful, even cheerful.

In the fall, I attended a retreat at Adelynrood called SoulCollage. This was a program based on Seena B. Frost's method of self-discovery, whereby you take five-inch by eight-inch cards and clip out pictures from magazines to put on the cards in a collage manner. The pictures don't have to be of anything specific, but rather images that appeal to you or resonate in some way. You create cards that reflect work, health, community, spirituality, and other pieces of yourself. To me, it felt like journaling, but in a visual way. I did a collage about nursing, one about the Blessed Mother, and even one about my arthritis. Each card, when finished, can tell you something about the subject matter. It's a way for a person to tap into their inner wisdom and the committee-like voices that each person has, the inner critic, the inner artist, the inner dreamer, and so on. I found it a fascinating exercise.

I attended a watercolor retreat, too, at the Marie Joseph Spiritual Center. This was a retreat run by an art therapist who worked at an air force base with groups of soldiers coming back from Afghanistan and Iraq with PTSD. Art therapy was a way for them to express themselves through their paintings, the unconscious processes captured in color and form. I found that there was no hiding one's emotional state in art therapy. Through the art, the psyche of the artist comes through. Starting with that year, I would make the art therapy retreat an annual thing. Many of my early paintings were dark and painful to look at. It was a continuation of me processing my grief over the sexual abuse scandal in the Catholic Church and my physical pain that was a part of that response. The act of painting and discussions with the retreat leader and fellow art participants would ultimately help my healing. Each year, as reflected in my art, I would become more positive. In the fourth year, to my surprise, the leader of the group would introduce mask making, which, of course, I was familiar with. This time around, the difference would be stunning. With Rachael, shortly after Robin's death, I had made a mask so dark that Rachael had to cover it with a towel. Now I made bright, colorful masks with stars and glitter, hearts and butterflies.

But then in 2007 came a bombshell. On a routine mammogram, it was determined that I had breast cancer. It was at a very early stage, but, naturally, it was terribly disconcerting. I had a lumpectomy and radiation and was told that, with both, I had a ninety-three percent chance of recovery. With chemotherapy, the prognosis increased to ninety-six percent. For the sake of three percent, I decided against the chemo and its side effects, focusing on healthy, holistic practices instead, like yoga, which I had started. I fully recovered, but the experience brought to me a deeper appreciation of life.

Shortly after I was diagnosed, I decided I needed to write a letter to my mother. It seemed like she should know. And although my chances were good, I couldn't help but think back to that homily that asked the question of what you would do if you had six months to live. Perhaps, I thought, it was time to try to connect once more with my mother. I called Brenda first. I didn't have our mother's address. Asking Brenda for it, I assumed she'd be pleased that I was trying to reconcile with our mother. Instead, Brenda angrily told me she didn't want to be placed between us. Worse, she said our mother would not want to hear from me. She wrote me a letter not long after trying to further explain, saying my request was unfair and unjust and that it should be up to Mother to decide whether I should have her address. I wrote back telling her that I believed discussing reconciliation with our mother would have brought her happiness. "Obviously, your angry response to me on the phone demonstrates how complex and wounded our relationship is," I wrote. "Thank you for discussing this issue with Mom and giving me her answer." Today, my sister and I exchange Christmas cards and that is more or less the extent of our relationship. I never did write a letter to my mother.

In 2010, Tom retired. Used to working long hours all his life, the adjustment wasn't easy for him. Plus, it seemed most of our friends were younger and still working. We'd made friends with other parents, as couples frequently do, but I'd had Grace when I was thirty-five. We hadn't realized it until Tom retired, but we were always the older couple. For Tom, it seemed strange, being retired when everyone else was still going off to work every day. It was a hard adjustment and it depressed him. He started drinking a little more and I found myself joining him.

But we'd never forgotten our neighbors coming back from their Florida vacations and soon Tom and I began spending winters in the Sunshine State, which helped us both. I could take off January through March and those months in the warm weather lifted my winter mood tremendously. Tom and I felt like newlyweds again. It was wonderful to see him happy.

One year in Florida, we took a genealogy course and I began looking back at where I'd come from. This prompted me to contact Aunt Martha, my father's sister, who was in her eighties and living in Ohio near my cousin Matthew. We went to visit her and this was when I learned more of my father's childhood, including the tarp that served as the roof over their heads and the times he'd walk out of the candy store without making a single purchase. This was when she gave me the details of the wedding, too—the fact that my father's parents didn't attend, and the fact that my mother had cried. She showed me her huge photo album book and I was able to see childhood pictures of myself. I'd seen very few. She allowed me to make copies of them and I was able to take them with me.

I finally retired at the age of sixty-five, and, after I had been cancer-free for five years, Tom and I decided to move to Florida full time. It was hard for me to leave my friends and our daughter, but I knew how much Tom loved Florida. I owed it to him. He'd always been there for me and it was my turn to be there for him. Besides, I'd received a sign. In Florida one day, after praying for guidance, I went for a walk with Tom. Over a rise in front of us soon came two sandhill cranes, a male and female. They walked right by us and it seemed to me as if the universe was telling me to make Florida our home.

Besides our old neighbors, we knew other people who had moved down and so we had some connections. I gave up drinking for good a year or so after the move. For one thing, I noticed my memory getting worse, and, at one point, I was even evaluated for dementia. What I found was surprising: Thankfully, I didn't have dementia. I had ADD. I'd had it all my life without knowing it and this explained my struggles in school. The drinking was making it worse, just one more reason to quit.

The move to Florida turned out to be a wonderful decision. Today, the sun is warm and welcoming and fills my heart with peace. We joined a church with a lot of social outreach programs, including a food pantry, financed by the church gift shop. The church supports a medical clinic and there are programs for seniors and others. There's a large choir in which I sing. With my work schedule, I hadn't been in a church choir since childhood and yet it was something I always wanted to do. I still travel north for the mothers group retreats, journaling retreats, and art retreats, plus for a couple of months in the summer to see friends and family. Peace of mind is, of course, an ongoing process. Besides my own history, I find myself often thinking about the abuse in the Catholic Church, as well as abuse that has come to light within other venerable institutions, like the Boy Scouts. It reaches into our schools and universities. Nothing seems safe. Predators are many and child sexual abuse is nothing less than an epidemic. Part of my charitable giving is for survivor support resources. And I pray for societal awareness, as well as for those who have the courage to come forward and say something. I pray the Catholic Church will, finally, step up, take the lead, develop new policies, and be a model for how to protect women, children, and men from sexual abuse. I pray for experts— psychologists, sociologists, researchers, university departments—to explore and investigate the causes of sexual abuse and find ways to prevent it or, at the least, better help the victims.

I pray for healing. Mine has reached a point that, at one time, I would not have thought possible, considering where my long journey started. Now, in the winters, there are no longer menacing moonlight shadows on the winter snow, but welcoming shadows from the swaying palm trees of my Florida home.

Clearing everything out of our house of thirty-five years for the move to Florida was something of a challenge, and I had to hire an organizer to help me decide what to keep and what to toss, where to keep my valuables safe, and how best to pack for the moving company. In my jewelry box, I came upon my Miraculous Medal, the medal commemorating the apparition of the Blessed Virgin Mary to Saint Catherine Labouré, the medal I had found lying in the grass around our house as a little girl. I had always hoped, when I found it, that it was meant for me, a blessing by which to help give me the strength I would ultimately need to escape the horrors of my childhood, a journey that took a lifetime.

I cradled the medal in my hand. I realized I had never worn it. When I found it, I needed to keep it hidden so my father wouldn't find and destroy it. When I was older, the arthritis in my neck made it too heavy to wear. Looking at the medal, I reflected on my life—a human journey, a spiritual journey. It was a journey of endless twists and turns. I was amazed and grateful that, even in my deepest despair and confusion, when I thought I was totally alone, I could now see there had been a positive energy and guiding presence supporting me. I thought about all the people who had come into my life—Dr. Mac, Tom and Grace, Joan, friends, and so many others. And I thought about the retreats and therapies and groups that had come along when

I needed them. My life had been filled with more love and blessings than I could have ever imagined. It was the paradox of the thorns and the rose.

I donated the medal to the religious table at our church for the Christmas fair. Somewhere, there was a person who needed a miracle, just as I'd needed one. There was another miracle left in that medal, I was sure of it. There's always one more miracle.

RESOURCES FOR SURVIVORS

The bIRch House
A supportive community dedicated to healing for female adult survivors of incest and childhood sexual abuse through programs, resources, education and advocacy
www.birch-house.org
781-316-0063

Rape, Abuse, and Incest National Network
National anti-sexual violence organization
Confidential 24/7 hotline
www.rainn.org
1-800-656-HOPE (4673)

Darkness to Light
Non-profit committed to empowering adults to prevent child sexual abuse
Confidential 24/7 hotline
www.d2l.org
1-866-FOR (367)-LIGHT (54448)
or text LIGHT TO 741741

The Courage to Heal: A Guide for Women Survivors of Child Sexual Abuse
by Ellen Bass and Laura Davis (4th Edition, 2008, New York: HarperCollins)
Often referred to as the bible of healing from child sexual abuse

Survivors of Incest Anonymous
Self-help peer support program guided by a set of 12 suggested
steps, promises, and traditions
National/international network of groups, including meetings
online and by phone
www.siawso.org
1-877-SIA (742)-WSO1 (9761)
or email contact form online

The Courage to Heal Workbook: A Guide for Women and Men
by Laura Davis (1990, New York: HarperCollins)
The companion volume to *The Courage to Heal* with survivor check-
lists, exercises, and activities

Guided Meditations for Trauma, Post-traumatic Stress, Depression,
Anxiety, and Panic
by Belleruth Naparstek ACSW, BCD
www.healthjourneys.com
1-800-800-8661

*Trauma and Recovery: The Aftermath of Violence from Domestic Abuse
to Political Terror*
by Judith Herman, MD (2nd Edition, 1997, New York: BasicBooks)

The Body Keeps the Score: Brain, Mind, and Body in the Healing of Trauma
by Bessel van der Kolk, MD (2014, New York: Penguin Books)

RESOURCES FOR PARTNERS, FAMILY, AND FRIENDS

Rape, Abuse, and Incest National Network
National anti-sexual violence organization
Confidential 24/7 hotline
www.rainn.org
1-800-656-HOPE (4673)

Darkness to Light
Non-profit committed to empowering adults to prevent child sexual abuse
Confidential 24/7 hotline
www.d2l.org
1-866-FOR (367)-LIGHT (54448)
or text LIGHT TO 741741

Partners in Recovery: How Mates, Lovers, and Other Pro-Survivors Can Learn to Support and Cope with Adult Survivors
by Beverly Engel, MFCC (1991, Los Angeles: Lowell House)

Allies in Healing: When the Person You Love Was Sexually Abused as a Child
by Laura Davis (1991, New York: HarperCollins)

Families in Recovery: Working Together to Heal the Damage of Childhood Sexual Abuse
by Beverly Engel, MFCC (1994, Los Angeles: Lowell House)

GRATITUDES

My journey has been a long one. Looking back, which the writing of this memoir has forced me to do, I see many, many people whose presence in my life helped guide me forward. I would not have made it without each and every one of them. Some know who they are. Others would have no idea, but if you're out there, and you recognize yourself somewhere in this book, understand that some small kindness you did for me, or some encouragement you spoke to me, or some small prayer or wish that you made on my behalf, made a difference.

Specifically, I need to thank my husband of forty-one years and our daughter for their love, and for always being there for me and giving me reasons to go on. The value of your support and your patience has simply been immeasurable.

Tom's extended family and some members of my extended family have provided me a love and belonging that I could not have gotten anywhere else.

I have many therapists, counselors, group leaders, spiritual leaders, teachers, and other professionals to thank. Too many to name here. But I would be remiss if I did not take this opportunity to at least thank Dr. Mac, whose care and wisdom are forever in my heart, and Joan, whose care and wisdom continue to amaze me. I would not have made it without either. Remarkably, all of the professionals from whom I was blessed to receive help came along at the precise right times in my life.

All the members of the groups I have become a part of have all, in one way or another, contributed to my healing. I only hope I somehow contributed to yours.

The many friends and work colleagues I have had the honor to know in my life have all deeply enriched me. I am the better for you all. Thank you.

I have mentioned many extraordinarily helpful books within these pages and I am immensely grateful for the insights, guidance, and work of all of the many authors.

Thanks, finally, to my co-author, Jerry Payne. I still don't know how we took my stacks upon stacks of journals and turned them all into a book! The process has been healing in and of itself. Thanks for your patience, dedication, professionalism, and skill.

Did you enjoy *Moonlight Shadows on the Winter Snow*?

If you found it helpful, and you feel others
might find it helpful, please help get the word out.
Consider leaving a review on Amazon.com, Goodreads,
Barnes & Noble, or wherever you purchased the book.

Connect with Sarah at *www.moonlightshadowsbook.org.*

CPSIA information can be obtained
at www.ICGtesting.com
Printed in the USA
LVHW030927240222
711901LV00003B/209